Football Research in an Enlarged Europe

Series Editors
Albrecht Sonntag
ESSCA School of Management
EU-Asia Institute
Angers, France

Dàvid Ranc
ESSCA School of Management
EU-Asia Institute
Angers, France

This series will publish monographs and edited collections in collaboration with a major EU-funded FP7 research project 'FREE': Football Research in an Enlarged Europe. The series aims to establish Football Studies as a worthwhile, intellectual and pedagogical activity of academic significance and will act as a home for the burgeoning area of contemporary Football scholarship. The themes covered by the series in relation to football include, European identity, Memory, Women, Governance, History, the Media, Sports Mega-events, Business and Management, Culture, Spectatorship and Space and Place. The series will be highly interdisciplinary and transnational and the first of its kind to map state-of-the-art academic research on one of the world's largest, most supported and most debated socio-cultural phenomenona.

More information about this series at
http://www.springer.com/series/14987

Series Editor Short Preface

"The city is not a company!" On the cover photo of this book.

Do cities need sport mega-events? The question may be open to discussion, but the reverse is definitely true: without well-functioning urban areas with their administrative capacities and cultural attractiveness, economic potential and infrastructure, the oversized international sport events of our times would be impossible to organise.

Sport mega-events are produced by transnational organisations whose main purpose is no longer the disinterested promotion of the sociocultural activity for which they were created in the first place. They sell a premium product of the global entertainment industry to urban communities that have, like themselves, fully interiorised the neoliberal redefinition of 'the social' as fundamentally economic in nature. Their customers are city administrators who see themselves as 'managers', applying the concepts and techniques of 'place branding' and 'corporate identity', in order to 'position' their city on a competitive market.

They would be well advised to open the dictionary and look up the etymology of the noun 'city'. They would find that the term's Latin root 'civitas' refers directly to membership in a community, i.e. a social and political entity rather than an economic one.

After decades of neoliberal dogma, market-oriented thinking, and increasing commodification of urban space, a growing number of 'citizens' remind their administrators and elected officials that their city 'is not a company'. In an almost ironic twist, it is precisely the disproportionate costs and concessions imposed by the organisers of mega-events that result in increased awareness on 'citizenship' among local stakeholders.

The slogan used by activists in the city of Poznan around the European football championship 2012 is therefore an excellent cover epigraph for this book. It sums up, in a nutshell, the public debate triggered by the event and analysed in detail in this original anthropological study.

Albrecht Sonntag, series editor.

Preface

On the 30th November 2014, in the second round run-off of the local elections and after 16 years as the Mayor of Poznań, Ryszard Grobelny was replaced by Jacek Jaśkowiak. Grobelny was for the first time elected by the City Council in 1998, and then re-elected in direct elections in 2002, 2006 and 2010. In 2014 he received less than 41% of votes. Even a couple of months earlier, only very few saw it happening (Grupiński 2014), but contrary to most predictions and assumptions (Bartkowiak 2013), the opposition proved capable of joining forces, mustering energies and dethroning the perennial mayor. On Internet forums commentators declared that they would vote for anyone just to remove the now-former mayor from his post. This only intensified after the first round of the elections, when most of the opposition candidates asked their electorate to cast their vote for Grobelny's opponent, Jacek Jaśkowiak, a businessman formerly associated with citizens' initiatives. Jaśkowiak was backed by the Civic Platform (*Platforma Obywatelska*), the party also forming a ruling coalition in the state government. It used to support Grobelny before but recently distanced itself from his politics and eventually advocated for his opponent. Significantly, on the same local forums, voters stressed that they did not vote for the party, but for the candidate who was able to beat Grobelny – no matter who backed him at the time.

Before the elections, I discussed the possible outcomes with a journalist who wrote a lot about local politics. I asked him to try to describe the people who, in his opinion, had voted for Grobelny in successive elections. He summed up the now-former mayor's electorate as Poznań's "bourgeoisie": entrepreneurs with small or medium-sized businesses and representatives of big business, who shared a particular "mentality":

> [They] think that Poznań is the best place to live and that it is sabotaged and underestimated by Warsaw. Conservative . . . , they do not travel and don't want to change anything; they are bored with the discussion on cultural life, because they go to the movies or to the theatre a few times a year and accept the festival definition of culture, which satisfies their needs. Their existence revolves around shopping centres or cultural events such as football games . . . they drive cars between their workplace, the shopping mall and home, the latter preferably located somewhere in the suburbs.

A few months before our meeting, the local daily published an opinion given by the owner of a well-known jewellery company, Wojciech Kruk. At a discussion on the future of Poznań, Kruk was arguing that the city had always been conservative, and its citizens were family-men cherishing hard work and a quiet life, who preferred spending their afternoons "back home with their wives" rather than "strolling in the centre" (Kruk 2013). My interlocutor did not hide his dissent:

> Wojciech Kruk is the embodiment of the worst features of the citizens of Poznań . . . , backward-thinking, an inability to understand urban processes, obscurantism . . . he is also convinced that he is perfect and that any critique is criticism . . . He is proclaimed a member of the business elite and political lobby in the city – which is rather funny because he has never really achieved any success: he inherited a company whose position on the market he then lost [as a result of a hostile takeover on the stock market], without even realizing when and how this had happened! This fact is one of the absurdities of the public debate in this city. If Poznań proves to be a city of this kind, then let it perish as soon as possible.

Contrary to this contention, another interlocutor of mine, with whom I discussed the long-term governance of Grobelny, drew my attention to the great potential which lies precisely in this "bourgeois", or, as he preferred to call it, "middle-class" character of the citizens of Poznań:

The liberal, or neoliberal camp [governing in the city] resembles at least some of the views of the citizens . . . economic growth, prosperity, stories like these . . . but more and more people are starting to notice that this government has not been serving the middle class, the lower middle class . . . and in my definition of the citizens of Poznań ninety percent of them can been described as lower-middle-class: everyone has something, a house, a flat. Ninety percent of ownership in Poznań is private. *Everyone has something or wants to have something, which makes them middle-class mentally.* . . . And therefore . . . the left in Poznań has no chance, it has no backing. People deluded themselves that this Grobelny-Civic Platform system . . . would work for them, but it started to serve, or believe, in a certain vision of the city: that large business should come and invest, that a rising tide lifts all boats, which is rubbish, because even if it lifts all, some of them are lifted higher than others. . . . And people start to see this stratification . . . there is this great respect of power in Poznań, but this situation is changing slowly.

Change, as Clifford Geertz aptly noticed, "is not a parade that can be watched as it passes" (Geertz 1995: 4). Yet in Poznań, there was a watershed, or a significant turning point (cf. Narotzky and Besnier 2014) that decided the results of the local elections in 2014. Asked in an interview given a few days after the polling day about the major successes during his 16 years in office (Grobelny 2014), the stepping-down mayor answered that the crowning achievement of his governance was Euro 2012 – the European Football Championship hosted in Poznań in June and July 2012. When the interviewer pointed out that paradoxically after the tournament everyone was convinced that the mayor would win the next election without hindrance, Grobelny replied that it turned out the citizens always vote for the future, not for the past. However, as I will argue on the following pages, it is indeed the past, or, more precisely, the imagined past, which had a crucial impact on the citizens' votes. The story of Euro 2012 can be told as a story about the rise and fall of *Grobelism* – the type of politics and political vision embodied by Mayor Ryszard Grobelny (Wybieralski 2011; cf. Stryjakiewicz et al. 2010: 54), which turned its back on the local tradition that once brought it to life.

Acknowledgements

I would like to thank my colleagues from the project, especially professors Albrecht Sonntag and David Ranc from ESSCA, France and Michał Buchowski from AMU, Poland, as well as my supervisors, professors. Werner Schiffauer and Marion Demossier, for all the guidance I got from them during my research. I also thank my Family for constant love and support.

Contents

List of Figures

1

Anthropology of Mega-Events

While it is true that sport can be seen as a vehicle to transmit values and ideas, it can also become a great test of the credibility of those values. Bea Vidacs argues that although football in itself "cannot mobilize a population, it will act as a catalyst in situations where political discontent is already [present]" (2010: 113). The same can be said of so-called mega-events, defined as large-scale events of "a dramatic character, mass popular appeal and international significance" (Roche 2000: 1). Under the conditions of global competition for international capital and a result of rapid development in communication technologies, and in a similar way as large-scale engineering and architectonic urban development projects (henceforth, UDPs), mega-events have become valuable promotional opportunities for regional and national governments worldwide (Swyngedouw et al. 2002; Horne and Manzenreiter 2006; Lowes 2002; Hall 2006). They are also desired advertising sites and tools for international business. However, their growing significance for local strategies raises questions about their supposed benefits, and more importantly, of their beneficiaries. Although presented as national pride and an economic boost, they seem to be especially appealing to

© The Author(s) 2017
M.Z. Kowalska, *Urban Politics of a Sporting Mega Event*,
Football Research in an Enlarged Europe,
DOI 10.1007/978-3-319-52105-3_1

politicians and coalitions of business stakeholders (Flyvbjerg 2014: 9). Media coverage, most notably before the recent mega-events in Brazil and during the 2014 Winter Olympics in Sochi, allows all to see that the exclusivity of the mega-events' beneficiaries' club raises growing objections. *Who* exactly is the country (the region, the city) that benefits from hosting the Games?

The vast and growing research on UDPs increasingly criticizes and contests the logic of hosting mega-events. While doing so, it puts further emphasis on studying them with greater regard to local specificity. Bob Jessop draws our attention to the "interpersonal, inter-organizational and institutional embeddedness" of local projects, which determine their feasibility in the "existing structural constraints and horizons of action" (Jessop 1998 [2013]); Bent Flyvbjerg calls for "social scientists foregoing the attempt to build generic models of social behavior and instead situate their work in ongoing political struggles as they occur in specific context" (Flyvbjerg et al. 2013). However, although detailed and conducted locally, this research is largely focused on figures and procedures which prove the unequal distribution of costs and benefits from mega-events. My endeavour takes over where most of those accounts stop. I see ethnography as a suitable method to study the factors and forces which determine the particular character of a place and, following Susana Narotzky and Niko Besnier, "a precious instrument that draws attention to the historical production of specificity and its role in structuring differentiation" (2014: 5). After all, as Gavin Smith aptly notes, "regions are about the historical ways in which people relate to one another through the medium of and by the use of place" (Smith 1999: 162). This research is concerned with historically produced expectations, beliefs and local classification systems, which decide on how mega-events are being *embedded* in the local *knowledge*, and under what circumstances this embeddedness might be questioned.

On the empirical level, the goal of this book is to deliver a vivid and contextualized ethnography of a particular locale in a specific historical time. The European Championship for men's national football teams (henceforth, Euro 2012) was the first sport mega-event which took place in the eastern part of Europe after the end of the cold war. Even before UEFA's 2007 decision to grant the event to Poland and Ukraine, the tournament became a strategic undertaking in the country. It justified political and business alliances, validated infrastructural projects and public spending and was the main point of reference in official discourses and negotiations of Poland's identity and scalar repositioning (Brenner 2011). Analysed in the light of the economic and political turbulences in the region and beyond, it can also be seen as change of the course that the country had been on for twenty-five years since the systemic transformation in 1989. As I will demonstrate in the book, Euro 2012 marks a shift in Poland's post-transformational history. It opened up the space for extensive negotiations of meanings and legacy of not only the socialist past but also of the post-socialist modernization of the country.

The case of Poznań, a city of half a million inhabitants in western Poland, is particularly interesting given that from the late eighteenth century till the end of World War I it belonged to Prussia. This has a major influence on how the local tradition has been *articulated* (Clifford 2001) in various periods of the city's history. As I will show, it also played a role in the local reaction to Euro 2012. The focus on the historically developed reservoir of meanings and values lets me deliver what is an ethnographic and nuanced account of this local perception. This account aims at filling the gap in the studies on sport mega-events. It shifts attention from capital flows and networks of beneficiaries towards the environment in which they are *able* to operate, and asks *why* certain projects and alliances might work (or not work) in a given setting. To put in another way, it draws upon the interdisciplinary research conducted on mega-events, developing it in a more anthropological manner. It does so by moving beyond the tracking and criticizing of the inequalities which are produced and reproduced on account of UDPs, including international sport tournaments. Although this task is necessary, it does not go far enough. Dealing pragmatically with the social world, as James Ferguson notes, "means going beyond pious wishing for equality to ask how *in*equalities are socially institutionalized and whether some such models of institutionalization are politically or ethically preferable to others" (2014:155).

This brings me to the theoretical input of the book. Discussing the relation between football and identity within the field of social sciences has grown into a "minor industry" (Vidacs 2010: 18), devoted to describing all cases where sport either divides or unites people. However, sports mega-events, including football championships, have received relatively little attention from anthropologists, although Catherine Palmer has already suggested the discipline should move from Geertz' cockfight to mega-events as "major sites and sources of cultural imagination in the late twentieth century" (1998: 267). This title is an attempt to make an original anthropological contribution to the interdisciplinary field of studies on mega-events. Palmer's main argument that mega-events "offer privileged points of entry into the ways local populations are drawn into the production of global culture" (265) is one of the *raisons d'être* of this book. The understanding of culture on the following pages goes beyond popular culture or consumer markets and allows the dialectical relation between local and supralocal politics and the economy to be discussed. Simultaneously, multi-sited ethnography of a mega-event enables us to follow the negotiations of local identity and meanings that occur when a particular setting is exposed to global flows and attention. In the longer term, I am interested in "the question of how social movements can help us understand the way people express themselves and in so doing, shape their own agency; a question of the interplay between social participation and the forming of individual and collective identities" (Smith 1999: 116–17).

Readers interested in urban politics, policymaking and governmentality, regardless of their interest in sport, will find this book placing a strong emphasis on local traditions and interpretations. By referring to some classic anthropological concepts, such as Maurice Bloch's "linguistic rituals" (1975) and Marshall Sahlins' "mytho-praxis" (1983, 1985), I analyse how the local myths of resourcefulness were invoked in Poznań to embed an entrepreneurial urban strategy there (cf. Jessop 2013 [1997]) on both the social and the individual level. I discuss Euro 2012 as a consequence of long-term entrepreneurial politics and governmentality, which was enacted by a reference to the *articulated tradition* (Clifford 2001) of Poznań as an entrepreneurial city and its citizens as entrepreneurial selves. However, the very same tradition of resourcefulness was deployed to challenge the urban policies, including the organization of the mega-event. Contrary to the authorities' expectations, Euro 2012 triggered a discussion on the extent to which the large business- and leisure-oriented urban strategy and promotional campaign correspond to the local *knowledge* (Foucault 1997; Rose et al. 2006). I argue that understanding different local receptions of various capital and political flows is impossible without trying accessing this knowledge. It is essential in the analysis and comparison of cases worldwide, and in the subsequent discussion on the global future. Of course, this applies not only to mega-events but also to whatever "circus is coming to town". Yet it is not just scientific analysis which is at stake here. I would argue that not only anthropological but all scientific writing nowadays has been recognized as political engagement. Therefore, when not only observing but also criticizing global changes and their local outcomes, we should listen more often to what people make of them – and *why*. In the long term, this would answer James Ferguson's aforementioned call for dealing with the social world pragmatically. No critique and no solution proposed will change anything, if those senses are not taken into account.

The main difficulty in deciphering this knowledge lies in the fact that I myself have been part of it.

***

This book grew out of my previous interest in economic anthropology and the anthropology of policies and political leadership (cf. Shore 2014; Shore and Wright 1997; 2011; Wedel, Shore, Feldman and Lathrop 2005), and is both an example of studying-up (Marcus and Fischer 1999; cf. Nader 1972; Hess 1996) and anthropology at home (Jackson 1987). Although doing ethnography at home implies that some things might be easier to grasp, as Edmund Leach notices, "fieldwork in a cultural context of which you already have intimate experience seems to be much more difficult than fieldwork which is approached from the naive point of total stranger. When anthropologists study facets of their own society, their vision seems to be distorted by prejudices which derive from private rather than public experience" (Leach 1982: 124). After all, "cognition is the most socially-conditioned activity of man" (Fleck 1979 [1935]: 42).

Hence, researchers working "at home" tend to ignore facts which appear to them as obvious and natural, whereas they are institutionally conditioned

(Douglas 1986). Norman Fairclough argues that "institutional practices which people draw upon without thinking often embody assumptions which directly or indirectly legitimize existing power relations", and that those practices "appear to be universal and commonsensical (. . .) [as they] have become *naturalized*" (Fairclough 2001: 27; emphasis original). This ideological common sense works mechanically and invisibly: people are unaware that their justifications, opinions and choices are not natural but constructed. Therefore, the question arises of how we can reflect on our own society without referring to the classifications which have been set up by the social institutions that formulate all our ways of thinking and judgements, including moral ones, even if we remain aware that "the sense of a priori rightness of some ideas and the nonsensicality of others are handed out as part of the social environment" (Douglas, 1986: 10)? Even the greatest thinkers of all time, as Mary Douglas' example of Max Weber shows, tend not to see how judgements, moral choices and everyday practices are determined by the institutions that they belong to. Those institutions should be understood as forces, not things, "facilitating certain practices, often by means of 'order' and regulations, and, just as surely, preventing other practices, closing certain social spaces, and inducing disorder and deregulation" (Smith 1999: 10–11; cf. Douglas 1986). Douglas' contemporaries truly believed that they were the first generation not controlled by the idea of *sacrum* and fully independent of the old institutional limitations. The author argues that this common imagination only proves the power of the omnipresent market and its rules, which try to analyse all social relations in market categories and according to the theory of rational choice. To use the Gramscian concept, this is how real hegemony works: "it both plays on common sense and produces common sense: if effective, it provides the sense that what is happening is obvious, normal and natural. It is taken for granted" (Smith 1999: 242).

But even if while doing research one must be extremely scrupulous and question every assumption, guiding metaphor and logical operation which she would otherwise use instantly, without giving it a second thought (and even if this task cannot ever be fully accomplished, and the results are definitely not without flaws), I take my cue from Gavin Smith when he insists on bringing engagement back home (Smith 1999). I would argue that when the ethnographer is no more distanced from the people she studies – no matter if this distance has been previously "geographically real or intellectually constructed" (Smith 1999: 3) – and locality is not just the lived experienced of others but also the reality of the analyst herself (7–8), there is an even greater need to decipher the institutions which determine people's self-understanding.

Accessing those institutions which shape our own personal and social identity seems to be easier during moments of transition, and through the medium of discourse. The category of crisis is useful when describing the moment of rupture, "a breakdown in social reproduction, a mismatch between configuration of cooperation that used to 'work'" (Narotzky and Besnier 2014: 7). The crisis occurs when the commonsensical and natural character of the social order is called into question. It is probably most discernible on the level of language. As one of the founding fathers of critical discourse notes, language is a battlefield between discourses within social entities: any "ideological struggle pre-eminently takes place in language . . . Having the power to determine things like which word meanings or which linguistic and communicative norms are legitimate or 'correct' or 'appropriate' is an important aspect of social and ideological power, and therefore a focus of [such] struggle" (Fairclough 2001: 73–4). Hence, this endeavour is concerned to great extent with the interface between semiotic expressions and extra-semiotic social life and focused on studying official discourses and policies (which are in the scope of current political anthropology). After all, culture is "a field of discourse . . . an arena on which values, norms and patterns of cultural actors are constantly negotiated" (Schiffauer 1997: 148, after Buchowski 2012: 37–8).

Michel Callon lays out the performative character of discourses. The performative dimension of formulas (statements) results in adjustment (or actualization) of the world of the formula, "in such a way that it can be said that the formula describes and represents its world correctly" (Callon 2007: 321; cf. MacKenzie 2006), and that the world acts according to the formula. Callon calls this relation, after Deleuze and Guattari, an *agencement*, or assemblage (cf. Deleuze and Guattari 2009 [1972]). Sometimes, however, events take place that are incompatible with the assemblage, and this crisis causes "other worlds to proliferate"

(Callon 2007: 323). This crisis is defined as an "overflowing" (Callon 2007) or as counter-performativity (cf. MacKenzie 2006). Of course, Callon's argument primarily tackles the problem of economics and technical language, but if we apply this concept to a broader context, my interest would lie in finding out *why certain agencements work at all* and why they sometimes *stop working*.

Douglas Holmes argues that we should not only look at performative actions from a top-bottom and therefore deterministic perspective and rather see them as "unfold[ing] with the public across a communicative field" (2014: 25). He draws our attention to the fact that any *knowledge* is reproduced in dialectical relation to people's beliefs, sentiments and expectations (xi; 10). To stick with Callon's terminology, the agencement works only if *the formula is negotiated with its world* (over a communicative field). In this shifted perspective, the key question is to understand why formulas and *their* worlds succeed, i.e. what happens during communication, and what triggers Callon's overflowing (cf. Kowalska forthcoming).

When posing questions about the reasons behind the prevalence of certain knowledge in a given locality, I am also following people who seem to be most engaged in shaping it. Since "the charm and power of anthropological interpretation lies in the fact that it refers to what people do and say" (Buchowski 1997: 16), this research is first and foremost about self-understanding on the part of the people who played a vital role in the events of 2012 and afterwards. This is an essential part of an attempt to capture the processes of culture and meaning making, new knowledge production and, subsequently, creating new forms of social life (cf. Osterweil 2014). Marxist, Gramscian, Foucauldian and Bourdieuan traditions all point to the unequal distribution of knowledge and power and to the role which people with greater access to knowledge have in shaping it. Studying the *regime of truth*, therefore, one must come across "the terrain of the active production of identifiable hegemonic fields" (Smith 1999: 243). It must include "the agency of political actors – intellectuals, leaders, class fraction and emergent blocs – in attempting to form hegemonic fields" (Smith 1999: 229).

Contemporary multi-sited ethnography at home is more and more often conducted among influential political and economic actors (often depicted as elites). It requires the acknowledgement that "we are dealing with counterparts rather than 'others' – who differ from us in many ways but who also broadly share the same world of representation with us . . . [even if] it is perhaps disturbing to think that we are more like some managers of capitalism or some politicians that we would like to admit" (Holmes and Marcus 2005: 250–1; cf. Kowalska forthcoming). Although as an anthropologist I am taught to always question "the system", I have managed to learn not to look at political and business elites as "people out there" (Verlot 2001). The distance between them and me was reduced before my doctoral research, when I worked in banking and marketing in Poland and abroad. For the final two years, I was employed by one of the flagship companies in my home city of Poznań. This last job allowed me to get to know local business and political coteries, to understand the inner logic of this world and modes of daily communication – and to start long-lasting friendships. It was the latter which fired my curiosity for the *cultural* background of urban strategy and politics. Eventually, it also let me understand that all of us who were raised and are based in the city refer to the same local *knowledge*, which shapes and indeed is shaped by our beliefs and expectations.

On the practical level, it also enabled me to conduct the research among "flex nets", to use Janine Wedel's term (2011): flexible networks of people who shaped the discourse and decided on the praxis on account of Euro 2012. Wedel draws upon George Marcus' project of a multi-sited ethnography (Marcus 1998:90–4) as she insists on seeing the researcher's role not as fixed or stable but as highly dependent on changing and various access to the field. It is particularly relevant when studying elites. The concept of power, according to Wedel, is nowadays less defined by organization, and more by a network, and requires the rethinking of some key methodological tools of ethnography. This approach satisfies the requirements of doing research on urban politics. Bob Jessop points that "one should look well beyond city dignitaries to assess the involvement of a wide range of actors behind a collective project and the institutional factors that help to consolidate their support. These actors can include branches of the local and/or central state, quangos and hived-off state agencies, political parties, firms, consultancies, trade associations, chambers of commerce, employers' organizations, business roundtables, trade unions, trades councils, citizens' and community groups, voluntary sector organizations, public–private partnerships, local educational and religious institutions, new social movements" (Jessop 1998 [2013]). People engaged in discussing the *relevance* of Euro 2012 to the local knowledge – and subsequently making this knowledge more accessible to me as a researcher – act on different levels of political and business life and represent different political views. They are hardly a homogenous entity which would be easy to pin down. During my research I tried to reach and talk to people having different opinions and different access to power. In fact, most of them asked me not to reveal their names, but many will probably be able to identify themselves on the following pages. I gave them as much of a voice as possible. It is my conversations with them which guided me through the field site.[1]

---

[1] My fieldwork took place in years 2012–2014. This is when I conducted most of the interviews and talked with various people engaged in the discussion on the city's future; attended official and informal meetings; and, last but not least, participated in sports events. However, also after the end of this work, I was determined to listen to those locals who would usually say that "they are not interested in politics", so I kept on having endless conversations in shops, cafés and during family meetings. The stories written in the book are told by people I talked to during my research. I thank all of them for their time, patience and dinners they cooked for me when I was writing up my dissertation.

2

Between and Betwixt. Poznań in the Scalar Perspective

In June and July 2012, alongside Warsaw, Wrocław and Gdańsk, Poznań hosted Euro 2012, the UEFA European Championship for men's national football teams. The event was co-organized with Ukraine and as such was the first European football tournament held behind the former Iron Curtain. Initially, it was just an eccentric idea of a Ukrainian oligarch. Michał Listkiewicz, the former chair of the Polish Football Federation (*Polski Związek Piłki Nożnej*, PZPN), recalls that it was Hrihorij Surkis, the chair of the Ukrainian Football Federation and a businessman, who in March 2003 hit on the idea of organizing the European Championship and invited Poland to make a bid with Ukraine (Jak przyznali nam Euro 2012: 10–11). In April 2007 in Cardiff, UEFA announced that Poland and Ukraine had won the bid (beating Italy and a joint proposal from Croatia and Hungary). In September 2007, the Polish Parliament (*Sejm*) unanimously voted in favour of hosting the event in the country. It became one of the major undertakings in Poland post-transformational history, i.e. after 1989 and the transition from a planned to a market economy.

© The Author(s) 2017
M.Z. Kowalska, *Urban Politics of a Sporting Mega Event*,
Football Research in an Enlarged Europe,
DOI 10.1007/978-3-319-52105-3_2

By Poznań's authorities Euro 2012 was seen as a key modernization project, a mega-event indeed, which would determine local politics and discourse for years. This chapter aims to put the tournament in context, presenting it from the perspective of local historical and geopolitical conditions, which is indispensable when analysing the significance and the legitimacy of the event. But, as Gavin Smith notices, "the particularity of a place arises not only from its natural characteristics and its peculiar history, but also from magnetic currents of force and counter-force that arise through the present-day strategies and constraints of capitalists and policy-makers" (Smith 1999: 134). This is why the political discourse in Poznań cannot be analysed only in relation to the historical and systemic background of the place; it has to be positioned within the broad perspective of the "uneven spatialization of globalization" (Çağlar 2010: 115).

One of the currents shaping my approach is the scalar perspective, which allows me to talk about the dialectical relation between history and *articulation* of tradition (Clifford 2001) on the one hand, and global processes affecting the locality at a given time on the other hand. Poznań's scaling can be understood as a dynamic, "differential positioning of a city, which reflects both (1) flows of political, cultural, and economic capital within regions and state-based and global-spanning institutions, and (2) the shaping of these flows and institutional forces by local histories and capacities" (Glick Schiller and Çağlar 2011b: 7; Glick Schiller and Çağlar 2011c: 71–2). The city scale does not exist as such and it is "no more than the temporarily stabilized *effects* of diverse sociospatial processes" (Brenner 2011: 31). Those sociospatial processes of scaling and rescaling refer to the ordering and reordering "of sociospatial units within multiple hierarchies of power.... Taken together, the terms 'scaling' and 'rescaling' serve as a conceptual shorthand that allows us to speak of the intersection between two processes: restructuring, including movements of various forms of capital, and the reorganization of relationships of power between specific sociospatial units of governance. The term 'scalar positioning' refers to the intersection of restructuring and rescaling processes at the particular moment of time" (Glick Schiller and Çağlar 2011b: 6–7). Different histories determine different modes of action, and therefore similar scaling and rescaling processes in various historical and institutional backgrounds result in different ways of restructuring capital and different shifts of power (Glick Schiller and Çağlar 2011b: 8), and different "representations, legacies, and expectations" (Glick Schiller and Çağlar 2011c: 80).

In this chapter, I examine "the temporarily stabilized effects of diverse sociospatial processes" which intersected in Poznań at the particular moment of time.

Genius Loci: Eastern Energy, Western Style

Before the Championship, the city welcomed guests and prospective investors, depicting Poznań in the following way:

> Poznań is a place where the energy of the New Europe is merged with the civilization of the West. A metropolis with over half-a-million residents, Poznań is situated in the most economically developed region of Poland, closer to Berlin than to Warsaw. Poznanians can be counted on – they are well-educated, competent and welcoming.
>
> The city is focused on achieving success, grounded on a *1000-year tradition of competence*. The most ambitious of projects and the bravest of visions have a chance to succeed here. The state of Poland was born in Poznań and it was also the location of the Greater Poland Uprising, the only successful armed bid for independence in Poland and a proof of the *exceptional resourcefulness* of its citizens.
>
> The people of this metropolis also stand out in terms of their *spirit of enterprise, renowned for generations*. During the great economic crisis at the beginning of the 20th century, Poznań managed to establish itself as one of the biggest trading areas in this part of Europe (. . .) By both realizing professional challenges efficiently and spending our free time creatively, we can look on Poznań as a City of Work and a City of Play. (About the city, 2012, originally in English; emphases: mine)

This short extract from the city's promotional campaign illustrates how a particular image of contemporary Poznań is constructed in the official discourse. Drawing from selected moments from the city's history and referring to its "1,000-year tradition of competence", this rhetoric aims to present Poznań as an entrepreneurial metropolis "focused on achieving success". By locating Poznań "closer to Berlin than to Warsaw", this perspective implicitly emphasises the economic advancement of the region and its ambitions to strengthen its links with the West.

The tropes of "the energy of the New Europe" and "civilization of the West" were also brought up in the title of this chapter. "Poznań. Eastern Energy, Western style" is the name of the promotional campaign commissioned to the Ogilvy PR agency by the city of Poznań in 2010. It encompassed five Western European countries – Great Britain, France, Germany, Italy and Belgium – and aimed to increase the city's recognizability on the continent. It derived from the narrative which praises Poznań as a beneficiary of the situation where it serves as a bridge between two world of different virtues. This narrative clearly associates the West with civilization and development. The slogan cropped up several times during my conversations with the authorities, and variations on it can be found in various documents. Although it is supposed to emphasize the uniqueness of Poznań, it can also be seen as an indicator of the "borderline" condition of the city, which does not belong to the East (any more), yet still has to "catch up" with the West. To understand this positioning, we should analyse it in historical terms – while taking into account both the realness of history and its constructedness (cf. Smith 1999: 15).

The city's origins are dated back to the tenth century. According to the narratives surrounding the promotion of the city, it was located on old trade routes from the East to the West, and from the Baltic Sea to the South. It then thrived as a centre of trade and crafts, especially in the fifteenth and sixteenth centuries, when it became a vital economic, cultural and educational site in the region. The image of Poznań as a vibrant trade city is popular among the locals. One of my interlocutors from the City Hall justified the promotional strategy of Poznań as a city of business by referring to its *traditional* character. He recalled that when he played computer games as a kid he especially liked those which were based in medieval merchant towns. For a teenager as he was back then, they appeared to be representations of Poznań.

The second half of the seventeenth century and the invasions by Swedish troops started a period of wars, cataclysms and political maelstrom in the whole country, which eventually led to the Partitions of Poland. Despite the attempts at reforming the Polish–Lithuanian Commonwealth – a dual monarchy comprising Poland and Lithuania – the kingdom was divided between three neighbouring crowns at the end of the eighteenth century. As a result of that, Poznań and the Greater Poland region (*Wielkopolska*) were incorporated into Prussia in 1793 as the Grand Duchy of Posen; they remained part of the Kingdom of Prussia, and then of the German Empire for more than 120 years (from 1848 as the Province of Posen).

Traces of the Prussian regime are still visible in the city, particularly in the architecture and layout of the city centre. Moreover, as part of the Empire, Greater Poland benefitted from the rapid development of capitalism and industrialization in the nineteenth century. Irena Kado and Jerzy Kado demonstrate that it was under the Prussian regime that the process of industrialization of the city started, also thanks to the Polish capital, and the strong emphasis on "organic work" among the local community (Kado and Kado 1967: 20–1). Organic work (*praca organiczna*) was denoting the Polish positivists' belief that the efforts and energy of the nation should be devoted to labour, education and increasing the economic potential of the Poles, rather than to uprisings against the neighbouring empires. Local Polish elites were devoted to educational and economic development rather than insurrections, the latter being, according to them, the domain of the other parts of Poland under Partitions, those divided between Russian and Austro-Hungarian Empires. The local perception of uprisings would be therefore similar to that of Friedrich Engels, who wrote to Karl Marx in 1851 that "Poles are *une nation foutue*, a lost nation (. . .). [They] have never done anything in history except engage in brave, blatant foolery" (Lewis Bernstein Namier 1946: 22).[1] The Greater Poland Uprising, which led to liberating Poznań from the Prussian rule at the end of World War I, was – as we read in the extract from the city's promotional campaign quoted

---

[1] Interestingly, the "Polish case" was one of few matters the two did not agree on. Recently, Kevin B. Anderson (2010) emphasized this fact in his book *Marx at the Margins. On Nationalism, Ethnicity, and Non-Western Societies*. Chicago: Chicago University Press; see also review of it, "Marx for Poles" by M. Buchowski (2015).

above – "the only successful armed bid for independence in Poland and a proof of the *exceptional resourcefulness* of its citizens".

The Prussian influences in Poznań and Greater Poland are not, however, limited to the years of Partitions. The history of Poland, especially its western regions, from the beginning of the statehood is also the history of relations with its closest neighbour. The town of Poznań was founded under Magdeburg law long before the Partitions. Germans settlers moved to and worked in the region for centuries (the best known group are the *Bambrzy*, who, in the eighteenth century, moved to the villages surrounding Poznań from the area of Bamberg in Upper Franconia and integrated fully with the local community). Contrary to Wrocław (German *Breslau*) and Gdańsk (*Danzig*), which became part of Poland after World War II and where German inhabitants were replaced with Polish settlers, Poznań and the Greater Poland region have had a long tradition of blending Polish elements with the German ones (on the "local culture" and problems with the German past in Gdańsk see: Stacul 2014). The local dialect in Poznań – *gwara poznańska* – draws extensively on the German language.

After the victorious Greater Poland Uprising (1918–1919), Poznań became part of the Second Polish Republic and started to build its position within the newly reborn country. The medieval and renaissance merchant past of the city, the Prussian legacy and the tradition of "organic work" were now used as pillars upon which to construct the local identity. The flagship initiative of in the interwar Poznań was the General National Exhibition (*Polska Wystawa Krajowa*, PeWuKa), an international fair which took place in 1929.

The General Exhibition was organized in order to show the work which had been accomplished in the ten years since the re-establishment of the Polish State after the end of World War I (Znaniecki 1931). It was part of a series of gigantic propaganda events held in the early twentieth century all around the world, such as world exhibition in Paris in 1900, the 1904 World Fair in St. Louis, USA, the British Empire Exhibition at Wembley in 1925 or the International Exhibition of Modern Industrial and Decorative Arts in Paris in 1925, which were usually generously subsidized by the state. The majority of investment in Poznań, however, was financed by the city, and even before the event Poznań was up to its ears in debt. From April 1928 till the end of March 1929 the city took out loans of more than 44 million zloties. In March 1931 the city debt rose to about 80 million. Poznań was then second after Lublin as the city with the highest debt ratio (PeWuKa Bis 2014). In spite of these problems, the Exhibition was a great propaganda success and became a legend.

It acted as a sign of progressiveness and modernity of the young Polish statehood and as such was a mega-event of its time (cf. Kowalska 2016). In Poland, it established the image of Poznań as a truly European city and trade centre. The event initiated the city's long tradition of international exhibitions, also linking it with Western Europe in the communist system: Poznań International Fair (*Międzynarodowe Targi Poznańskie*) was the window to the big world and a source of great pride for Poznań's citizens. Although a financial failure, the General Exhibition was highly praised afterwards as a symbol of local virtues of resourcefulness and diligence. Interestingly, the first exhibition in Poznań was organized in 1911 by the Prussian authorities. It took place on the premises where subsequent fairs were held and where then the first Polish fairs took place in 1921. This infrastructural base was the main argument for organizing the General National Exhibition in Poznań, not in Warsaw.

At the beginning of World War II in 1939, Poznań was annexed to the German Third Reich as the Province of Warthegau. Several times attacked by the air force, from 1944 it became the arena of intense fights between the Reich and the Allied Forces. Heavily destroyed and plundered, the city was liberated by the Red Army in the Battle of Poznań in February 1945. It was to become part of a very different Poland – with shifted borders, a new communist government dependent upon the Soviet Union and masses of people forced to leave their lost homelands in the east and travelling to the formerly German territories in the west.

The new communist regime proved to be something of a revolution for the hitherto social structure and urban planning of the city. Central industrialization programmes ensured the economic development of the region, with new work and housing areas guaranteeing a population increase and the social advancement of the working class and migrants from poorer parts of the country. Even those authors who tend to see the communist period as a time of regress and isolation admit that due to the economic, social, administrative and educational development and its growing national significance, "at the time Poznań began to develop its metropolitan functions" (Stryjakiewicz et al. 2007: 31). It was after World War II in the period of centrally planned economy that Greater Poland (and the city of Poznań) was transformed from a predominantly agricultural region into an industrial one. In the past capitalism in Poland did not result in the creation of cities, but rather of industrial settlements; it did not stimulate urbanization but only industrialization. In Greater Poland it changed in the 1960s, when a strong relation between industrialization and urbanization could be observed (Kado and Kado 1967).

Having said that, the regime's flaws and limitations resulted in the political change of 1989, and a difficult economic and social transformation aimed at replacing the state command system with the free market. In 1989, Poland moved up a gear and focused on establishing close political and economic links with Western Europe. After Poland's accession to the North Atlantic Treaty Organization in 1994, and especially to the EU in 2004, the country speeded up the process of systemic European integration, also due to the use of a wide range of structural funds for investment and restructuration.

The modern image of Poznań has been built up in reference to a few key moments and periods in the city's history. People's self-understanding arises in a particular historical setting and in a given locality, and therefore ethnographic analysis of "what rabbit is produced out of the hat of the past" (Smith 1999: 146) is a *sine qua non* of anthropological research. Part of this research is the acknowledgement that power is typically legitimized by exploiting symbols of the past, which can be (positively) valued by the community (Kowalska 2017). Anthropology of political leadership puts emphasis on studying ways in which the past is *engaged* in legitimizing current political strategies and discourses. After all, "anthropologists and historians have become acutely aware...that 'culture' and 'tradition' are anything but stable realities handed down intact from generation to generation" (Hanson 1989: 890). Yet they must be presented as *characteristics* of the place in order to justify political praxis. Classic anthropological studies of power analyse how political leaders legitimize their position by referring to the supreme, eternal order. Maurice Bloch (1975) writes about the "linguistic rituals", i.e. the extensive use of allegories, metaphors and proverbs "which tend to be fixed, eternal and orthodox" in speeches given by the leaders of the Merina of Madagascar (15; cf. Shore 2014). Marshal Sahlins' discussion on mythopraxis also shows how local founding myths influence decisions and actions of contemporaries (1985). However, it is the application of those theories to the western social realities which seems the most interesting. Michael Herzfeld shows how through "monumentalizing the past" power-holders influence what should be remembered and what should be forgotten (2000: 234), and Marc Abélès scrutinizes François Mitterrand's use of political rituals (1988). The extract from the city webpage quoted at the beginning of the chapter exemplifies how certain qualities are presented in the official discourse as the *traditional characteristics* of the locality. Below, I analyse how the local tradition has been *articulated* (Clifford 2001) in the local discourses over years.

A valuable source of information about the city's past in the twentieth century and how it was reproduced over time are two relatively little known sociological surveys, one conducted in 1928 by Florian Znaniecki, and the other in 1964 by Janusz Ziółkowski. Although backed with two different theoretical approaches, both surveys invited the citizens of Poznań to answer a few questions about their city and as such were broadly advertised in various media (participation in both surveys was voluntary). These are great sources of information on how people felt about the city a decade after World War I, and then in the heyday of the People's Republic of Poland (*Polska Rzeczpospolita Ludowa*). The results and the comparison of the surveys were published together in 1984 in a volume edited by Ziółkowski and his colleagues and titled "What does the city of Poznań mean to you? Two surveys: 1928/1964" (*Czym jest dla Ciebie miasto Poznań? Dwa konkursy: 1928/ 1964*). Importantly, both surveys were commissioned by the city.

The main difference between the two undertakings, as the commentators argued in 1984, is the hierarchy of the raised problems: the younger generations were strongly focused on the issues of development and growth of the city (Znaniecki and Ziółkowski 1984: 15). What was

evident for the scholars comparing both surveys was the social advancement of the working class in the sixties, which grew from the most
socially underprivileged one of the mid-twenties to the hegemonic class
in the People's Republic of Poland (Znaniecki and Ziółkowski 1984: 17).
This social advancement was not only visible in the respondents'
answers: working class representatives comprised a significant per cent of
the respondents in the 1968 survey. The absence of business representatives in the same survey was not particularly surprising given the political
and economic context of the time, but representatives of industry and
wealthy commerce did not take part in the 1928 survey either (Znaniecki
and Ziółkowski 1984: 54). Notwithstanding certain changes, the authors
of the publication concluded that the image (and the self-image) of a
typical citizen of Poznań had not changed over the 40 years which
separated the two surveys, and they argued that it was due to the strong
influence of the particular *genius loci* of the city (Znaniecki and
Ziółkowski 1984: 18). I propose to look at this *genius loci* not as a fixed
"spirit of place", but as perpetually reconstructed image of the place. As
such, my understanding differs from that of the authors. The "spirit of
place" understood as a set of local characteristics does not exist as such – it
is produced and reproduced over the course of history. It should be more
understood as already mentioned "articulated tradition", which James
Clifford defines as "a kind of collective 'voice', but always in this constructed, contingent sense.... An articulated ensemble is more like a
political coalition or, in its ability to conjoin disparate elements, a cyborg"
(2001: 478).

The Institute of Sociology began its studies on Poznań when the city
was preparing to organize the first General National Exhibition in 1929.
It was suspected that the preparations for the event would influenced the
growth of interest in public affairs, and therefore the city magistrate and
the sociologists decided to conduct this "sociological experiment aimed
at revealing any development possibilities within civic society, i.e. the
social potential which could be used for the sake of the development of
the city" (Znaniecki and Ziółkowski 1984: 36). As such, the 1928 survey
aimed at finding out, in Znaniecki's words, "what are the pillars of the
community in the eyes of its inhabitants" (Znaniecki and Ziółkowski
1984: 48). Although the public response to the survey was relatively

poor – disappointed Znaniecki interpreted it (also elsewhere) as proof of his contemporaries' lack of interest in public affairs, and their passivity (Znaniecki and Ziółkowski 1984: 59; cf. Znaniecki 1931) – the whole endeavour resembles the very modern idea of an opinion poll. It offers the contemporary reader an insight into the process of negotiating the local identity in the pivotal interwar period.

Recalling the opinions and perspectives gathered by the sociologists serves here not only as a time machine: it enables us to track the evolution of certain features and tropes important in the process of shaping the local identity, first after regaining independence from the Prussian regime, and then under the new conditions of the command system and as part of the Eastern bloc. What, then, did the citizens of Poznań think of their city and themselves a decade after the end of World War I[2]? I will now give voice to the respondents of the 1929 survey.

> Poznań is a Polish city, it is not an international hell like Paris . . . it is quiet. I am a family man and I like the quiet life. Moreover, it is a healthy city . . . and very pleasant to the eye, clean and green. . . . This city has a great future ahead. (1928 survey: respondent no. 4, Znaniecki and Ziółkowski 1984: 85)
>
> I know other big cities in Poland . . . Poznań is distinguished among them mainly because it is a truly Polish city and because of the diligent character of its citizens. They maintain high western culture, combine moral life with civic duties and love national traditions. (1928 survey: respondent no. 5, Znaniecki and Ziółkowski 1984: 86)

---

[2] For the sake of the length of this book I will not refer to all threads which were raised in the surveys, however appealing they are, such as the presence and characteristics of the Jewish minority in the city before World War II, or the gender issue. The latter seems particularly interesting. There was a more equal gender proportion in the earlier survey than in the one conducted in 1964: the authors of the publication interpreted the "impressive" results of the 1928 research as an effect of the recent social and political emancipation of women, and their limited participation in the poll in 1964 as a reflection of the "natural" condition of women who, obviously now much more emancipated than their mothers and grandmothers, generally show little interest in politics and public affairs (Znaniecki and Ziółkowski 1984: 11–12). More information on these and other issues can be found in Znaniecki and Ziółkowski's publication.

Brought up in Prussian rigour, [the citizen of Poznań] has lost some of the Polish or Slavic shortcomings and obtained some very positive features, such as diligence, conscientiousness, thriftiness, loyalty in business, orderliness and shed laziness, unpardonable recklessness and quarrelsomeness. (1928 survey: respondent no. 4, Znaniecki and Ziółkowski 1984: 114)

There is a need for, a love of and practice of comfortable life in Poznan. Cleanliness, order and the solidity of buildings and some features inherited from the Germans have made Poznan a typical western city. . . . Gone is the impetuousness, quick temper and Slavic hastiness, and instead there is slow and deliberate calculation typical for the German middle class. Fighting Germanization taught people resilience, which is revealed in their patience and perseverance. (1928 survey: respondent no. 8, Znaniecki and Ziółkowski 1984: 115)

A typical citizen [of Poznań] is quiet, it is not easy to make his blood boil. . . he takes care of the family. . . is thrifty and diligent. . . gets up early and goes to bed early . . . he is very ambitious and has a good opinion of himself, and therefore has a long list of prejudices against people from other parts of the country. . . . (1928 survey: respondent no. 9, Znaniecki and Ziółkowski 1984: 113–14)

The 1928 survey takes one back to a very distinctive period in the city's history, challenging and difficult, but full of hope. After regaining independence and joining Poland, reborn as it was after World War I, Poznań found itself in a new economic and political situation, and had to define its stand and identity within and towards Polish statehood. The General National Exhibition became a symbol of the virtues of the citizens of Poznań, proved their diligence, entrepreneurial skills and belief in the value of honest and systematic work (cf. Znaniecki and Ziółkowski 1984: 118). Those features of their personality keep on coming back in the survey respondents' opinions. They see the city as clean and healthy, orderly and of high Western culture, and its inhabitants as diligent and good at business. The respondents' answers reveal their conviction that the character of the city and its citizens was defined under the Prussian rule: people learned that their existence and identity depend on hard work, not romantic uprisings, and through their focus on business and by absorbing "some elements of law, order and culture", they "become more German" than Polish, or Slavic. The Prussian legacy, therefore, obviously has both positive and negative dimensions. On the one hand, Poznań is seen as a "Polish city", a "stronghold protecting Poland against the German flood" (Znaniecki and Ziółkowski 1984: 285), while on the other hand, some characteristics which were supposedly acquired by the citizens of Poznań under Partitions, in the independent Poland were actually perceived as their greatest virtues (Znaniecki and Ziółkowski 1984: 288–96).

This identification has its flipside, as the respondents often define their peers as lacking *good* Polish features, as in the responses quoted below:

I've thought about the citizens of Poznan many times. I like their reliability. But why is it that they all are so slow and ponderous? Before they make up their minds on things which require fast decisions, it is already too late. Before merchants fetch a stylish fabric, it is not in vogue anymore; before cabmen harness their cabs, snow has already thawed out. . . . Sometimes the whole city appears to be a clock which the slightest movement could bring to a halt. . . . which goes slower and slower with its tick-tock, tick-tock. . . . (1928 survey: respondent no. 26, Znaniecki and Ziółkowski 1984: 117–18)

Very hardened in their life struggles, they do not see their brothers as neighbours: they are eager to do business together, but they lack the old Polish hospitality. (1928 survey: respondent no. 4, Znaniecki and Ziółkowski 1984: 114)

As for intellectual features, there is this organizational sense, some abilities, but they are somehow dormant due to the occupation. . . . German schooling did a lot of damage to Polish minds, people learned mostly by heart and did not develop in terms of their intelligence. This is the main reason why their minds are rather passive and dull. (1928 survey: respondent no. 9, Znaniecki and Ziółkowski 1984: 113–14)

One of the respondents, when discussing the post-war migration from the Eastern Borderlands (*Kresy*[3]), noticed that the presence of those

---

[3] *Kresy* in the survey referred to the far-east parts of the Second Republic (1918–1939), and, to some extent, the former Polish–Lithuanian Commonwealth, which were annexed to the Soviet Union after World War II. They are now part of western Ukraine, western Belarus and eastern Lithuania.

newcomers, people of "great bravery and fantasy", is beneficial to the native citizens of Poznań, "who know how to work, but not how to risk and fly" (1928 survey: respondent no. 9, Znaniecki and Ziółkowski 1984: 63).

To sum up, the citizens of Poznań saw themselves as hard-working and pragmatic, good at business and loving order (or *ordnung* in the local dialect, after German *Ordnung*) but, at the same time, lacking Slavic fantasy and openness. Thirty-six years later, the respondents of the 1968 survey described the citizens of Poznań in a very similar manner as those in the interwar survey. The Faculty of Sociology at the Adam Mickiewicz University asked a very similar question in the open survey titled "What does the city of Poznań mean to you?" (*Czym jest dla Ciebie miasto Poznań?*). Those who responded this call saw themselves as "diligent and disciplined" (1964 survey: generation I,[4] Znaniecki and Ziółkowski 1984: 198), with a strong reverence for the "virtues of order, scrupulous work and honesty" (1964 survey: generation III, Znaniecki and Ziółkowski 1984: 199) and "upright" (1964 survey: generation II, Znaniecki and Ziółkowski 1984: 295). Some of the respondents, like those in 1928, point to the "dark side" of this favourable picture, as does this woman, who criticizes the myth of Poznań as an exceptional city:

One of the characteristics of this urban mythology is . . . its uniqueness in relation to other Polish cities. . . [whereas people's] positive characteristics . . . are in fact derived from rather negative features. Hence, reliability favours the lack of fantasy and imagination, law and order – bureaucratic servilism and autarchy – parsimony and selfishness. (1964 survey: generation II, Znaniecki and Ziółkowski 1984: 200)

---

[4] The coding used in the 1964 survey was different to that used in 1928, where it was numerical. Now, 133 respondents were divided in three groups, represented by categories: generation I (born during the Partitions or World War I), generation II (born in the interwar period or during World War II) and generation III (born in the People's Republic of Poland). Most of the respondents were originally from Poznań or Greater Poland, 22% migrated to the city from elsewhere (11%: no data was provided); the majority of them had secondary or higher education; women to men ratio was 38 to 95.

The most frequently mentioned virtues and flaws of Poznań's citizens were summarized by the authors in a chart (Znaniecki and Ziółkowski 1984: table 33, 300–1). According to it, the most distinguishing features of the citizens would be diligence and perseverance; conscientiousness, reliability and sense of duty; thriftiness; resourcefulness; love and attachment to the city; and cleanliness, tidiness and order. The respondents often referred to local traditionalism and conservatism, common sense, social discipline and organizational flair. Of course, this chart of positive characteristics should be seen as part of the *politics of articulation* of a certain image of the locals. The rest of Poland can question this self-definition. For instance, they usually see the citizens of Poznań as stingy, not frugal. What may be seen by others as a fault is for Poznanians proof of their entrepreneurial skills.

When respondents talked about the main functions of the city, the majority voted for economic ones (especially industry and trade, with a strong emphasis on the role of the International Fair); next, for scientific and education ones, and less often for cultural ones. Poznań was usually perceived as a city of trade and business, and as an academic centre; other functions were less frequently mentioned (Znaniecki and Ziółkowski 1984: 280). Very often those functions and features were linked with the Prussian legacy of the region. This is particularly relevant when one realises that after 1945 the city and the whole country became part of the Eastern bloc and their politics was officially reoriented towards the East. The Prussian past, to a large extent determining the character of the city, and the role of the International Fairs also connected Poznań with the West in the communist era.

Three leitmotifs can therefore be identified in the respondents' opinions, both in 1928 and in 1964. All seem integrally linked with the local identity: the Prussian legacy with its reverence for *Ordnung*, the tradition of the organic and dissent work rather than of engagement in insurrections; and entrepreneurial skills, whose origins could be traced back to the city's medieval history, and which apparently developed and thrived in the early-capitalist environment in the German Empire (cf. Karwowski 2005).

A picture of the more contemporary Poznań is drawn by the geographers from Adam Mickiewicz University, who between 2006 and 2010 analysed the creative potential of the region while working on a European research project ACRE: Accommodating Creative Knowledge – Competitiveness of European Metropolitan Regions within the Enlarged Europe. The project's goal was to assess the impact of the emerging "creative class" on competitiveness in Europe and to find out which regions have the potential to develop as "creative knowledge regions", and which rather not. Two project publications are most relevant to our discussion at this point: "Poznan faces the Future. Pathways to creative and knowledge based regions" (2007) and "Policies and strategies in Poznan. How to enhance the city's competitiveness" (2010). The findings and prognoses presented there are partly based on analysis of strategic municipal documents and media discourse, and on interviews with local authorities. While describing the global position of the city, the authors emphasize the discontinuity of the city's development due to the "inability to keep up with global processes under the communist system", which is also the reason why the city's "metropolitan functions are not fully formed yet" (Stryjakiewicz et al. 2007: 1; cf. Stryjakiewicz et al. 2010: 3). Their perspective is growth and modernization oriented, and they are concerned about what should be done to connect Poznań with the European network of creative metropolises, and make it a competitive city on the global capitalist market. When saying that "in Poland (and in the other post-communist countries) many socio-economic and spatial processes, including the emergence of a creative class and creative industries, generally lag behind those in Western Europe" (Stryjakiewicz et al. 2007: 2), they refer to the developmental rhetoric of "catching-up" with the West. Having said that, they insist on local strategies not imitating or copying western ideas, but rather drawing on local traditions and strong points. Those strong points are expressed in economic terms, which exemplifies the entrepreneurial strategy for the city's development: Poznań's economic profile is diversified, the city finances are well managed, municipal institutions are efficient and enjoy success in attracting foreign investment to the city. The authors also refer to "the historically developed features of human capital: entrepreneurship and a high standard of work" (Stryjakiewicz et al. 2007: 1–2), which distinguish Poznań from other cities in the country. They quote Ziółkowski, whose opinion they seem to share, that the citizens of Poznań are "perhaps less spontaneous and extro-verted [than people elsewhere in Poland], but are very reliable and hard-working" (after: Stryjakiewicz et al. 2010: 17–18). Like the respondents of the sociological surveys from 1928 to 1964, these geographers put emphasis on economic and business character and the potential of the region.

The short outline of the history of the city which the authors present is an interesting example of producing an image of Poznań as a prosperous and entrepreneurial city, and its inhabitants as diligent and efficient citizens. In this narrative, the Prussian regime is seen as beneficial to the city, for "despite the restrictive policy of the occupiers, in the 19th century Poznań's scientific and economic life flourished thanks to the operation of Polish institutions and private enterprises. They competed successfully with Prussian firms, and to do this the city residents had to muster up their dormant resources of creativity and entrepreneurship" (Stryjakiewicz et al. 2007: 3). Despite the obstacles and attempts of Germanization, as the authors stress, Poznań's cultural life thrived under the Prussian regime: the Polish community was able to erect buildings which have since become cultural symbols of the city, they published books and journals, and devoted themselves to "organic work", economic devel-opment in the whole region. After the unification of Germany and introduction of Bismarck's anti-Catholic *Kulturkampf* policy, those conditions became, to say the least, less favourable for the Polish citizens of the city. Although Poles suffered from oppressive mea-sures and discrimination since the region was annexed to Prussia, it was under the Iron Chancellor when Germanization aimed at eradi-cation of the Polish nation intensified. On the other hand, Poznań, as the furthest east of the Prussian strongholds, was not passed over by the more conducive winds of history. At the end of the nine-teenth century, it had adapted to the new conditions of the capitalist economy and grown as a vibrant centre of the agricultural processing industry, metallurgy and equipment construction. Those changes, which took place much more quickly in Germany than further to the south-east of Europe, resulted in the region's advancement in comparison with two other parts of Poland – one under Russian, the other under Austro-Hungarian rule – which were soon about to unite after Partitions (Stryjakiewicz et al. 2007: 28). A particularly impressive example of the differences between the "two Polands" – formerly German Poland A and Poland B, consisting of former Russian and Austrian parts (underinvested by the two empires) – is the map of Polish railways. Very dense in the west and much sparser in the east, this network has not changed much in almost 100 years since the end of World War I.

My interlocutors also often stressed the German-like character of Poznań and the entrepreneurial profile of its citizens. They emphasized the economic potential of the region and the merchant and business character of the city. Most of them referred to *Ordnung* as a distinguishing characteristic of the city and often used the locally popular prover of a German origin: *Ordnung muss sein*, "there must be order". This is why activities which are not ordered and economically rational raised certain objections among many of them, as I will demonstrate.

The interwar mayors of the city, Jarogniew Drwęski and the legendary Cyryl Ratajski (the "father" of the General National Exhibition), were often recalled by my interlocutors as exemplary politicians. One of the city councillors I talked to called them his "role models" and "personal heroes". He also added:

> Of course, I cannot forget about those working people, the community's political and social workers and activists, who remained active in the territory annexed by the German Empire and engaged in organic work, which is the best example of our creativity. Because, contrary to what some media say, we are and have always been very creative. Obviously, it depends on the individual, but those people's histories prove that we are pragmatic, but also inventive, creative, able to work under German occupation and still focused on one goal, which was independence, and this is what I really like, this is an example of long-term thinking, looking for common denominators among people . . . they all put their stamp on this place (. . .). Poznań is different to Galicia, which is creative but lacks our pragmatism, different to Warsaw, where you have to fight your way through, and different to Wrocław, still building up its position. We will never be a second Barcelona, but we do not have to be worse than Leipzig or Dresden – we have the same potential.

It is not especially surprising that this councillor talked about two German cities as examples to follow. The Prussian presence left a strong imprint on the region, to the extent that some of my interlocutors admitted that they feel more at home in Berlin than in Warsaw, the German capital being just a "bigger Poznań" to them.

Yet it was the interwar period which became the Golden Age in the negotiations of the local identity in the years preceding and on account of Euro 2012. With the legendary General Exhibition as the landmark event, the years 1919–1939 are associated with prosperity and development. In independent Poland the city made use of its potential and strengths, progressively building up a strong position within the new statehood. Stryjakiewicz et al. also claim that after regaining independence, the creative potential of the city blossomed: the region developed dynamically, which was, as the authors argue, "due to the entrepreneurial skills of Poznan citizens, who established companies and opened new workplaces" (Stryjakiewicz et al. 2007: 28–9). This was only interrupted by the outbreak of World War II in 1939.

In contrast, the post-war communist period is usually perceived as a time of imposed power and developmental regression, although Poznań "was lucky to avoid becoming a heavily industrialised city and had developed commercial functions" (Stryjakiewicz et al. 2007: 2–3). The geographers' unfavourable perception of the communist era is by no means exceptional. My interviewees also differentiated between the glorious interwar period and communism, the latter brightened only by the presence of the International Fair, but overall "a state of both structural and political-cultural backwardness . . . as well as socio-economic stagnation" (Giordano 2009: 300; cf. Kowalska 2016; 2017). A civil servant claimed in our conversation that

> The interwar period had a crucial impact on the development of the city. But also in the post-war period, between 1945 and 1979, when Poland was a closed country, Poznań had its International Fairs. This was a window to the world, the whole country looked at Poznań and knew that this is where the whole world meets, and this is why at the beginning of the 90s we were at a very different level than Wrocław, Gdańsk or Szczecin.

As Christian Giordano observes, "the fifty-year period prior to 1989 has been portrayed nearly always as an abnormal hibernation phase or an imposed deviation endured by these societies during their natural advance towards 'progress'" (2009: 299; cf. Nagengast 1991; Dunn 2004; Stacul 2014; Mokrzycki 2001; Buchowski 2012; Jasiecki 2013). But even in the post-war, communist period, Poznań is considered by contemporaries slightly different to the rest of the country, more western. It was the post-transitional years, however, which reopened the region to Europe and gave hope for its desirable growth: new conditions "allowed the *rebirth of entrepreneurship* and organisational skills among the residents of Poznan and *restored the city to its traditional 'external openness'* connected with its commercial and communication functions" (Stryjakiewicz et al. 2007: 3; emphases: mine). Clearly, what the authors suggest here is that the transition from a command to a market economy was getting back on the right track. This exemplifies the processes of reimagining the city's *genius loci* and embedding the systemic change in the local context. In the new system, the "natural" skills of the city's inhabitants could flourish. As if to confirm it, the authors add that the post-transformational urban growth, linked with "securing the rules of a market economy and the processes of privatization and commercialization" (Stryjakiewicz et al. 2007: 91), resulted in a rapid increase in the number of new private businesses (Stryjakiewicz et al. 2007: 32), which enabled the city to undergo transformation into a service-dominated economy.[5] Year 1989, therefore, seems to mark the restart of the modernization process which was interrupted in 1939 and neglected (if not reversed) in the communist era: "this meant replacing the old command system which organised the structure and functioning of the state, society and economy with one in which the regulatory role was played by the laws of economy and social development" (Stryjakiewicz

---

[5] The dominant sector in the city's economy is the service sector, which accounts for 70.9% of the region's gross value added. Small business (with under 10 employees) constitute more than 95% of the total number of firms in what is termed the "creative sector", but it is the large foreign corporations (e.g. Volkswagen, GlaxoSmithKline Pharmaceuticals, Bridgestone and Beiersdorf) that have invested a total of 12.5 billion zloties ($4.3 billion) and ensure the transfer of advanced technologies and innovations to the city (Stryjakiewicz et al. 2007: 52).

et al. 2007: 5). Stryjakiewicz's view of the post-1989 period is favourable: the country's economy becomes modern, market oriented and effective, with a large number of business now in private hands and/or being the result of direct foreign investment, the latter perceived as crucial in the process of modernization. What is characteristic is that the authors explicitly state that "the formation of a modern society – well-educated, full of initiative, active, creative, and responsible – will take much longer, at least 20–30 years" (Stryjakiewicz et al. 2007: 6), and that "it should be kept in mind . . . that Poland is still in the middle of constructing a new reality for itself, which is a task hard to complete successfully given the legacy of communism" (Stryjakiewicz et al. 2007: 7–8).

In the official narrative, the years between 1945 and 1989 are seen as a gap in the process of development. This is confirmed in other research on the region. As Édouard Conte and Christian Giordano write, such a view exemplifies a unilinear vision of history. Communism is seen as a historical aberration, whereas the passage to post-socialism "represents a 'return to the future' in that the conversion to capitalism . . . purports to restore a *status quo ante*" (Conte and Giordano 1999: 6).

Modernization of the region started under the Prussian regime and thrived in the interwar period, drawing on local resources and the predispositions of the people of Poznań. Although some argue that the beginnings of private entrepreneurialism in the whole country should be traced back to the 1970s, this does not affect the local historical narration, i.e. the articulation of the entrepreneurial tradition (cf. Nagengast 1991; Stacul 2014). The years after World War II seem to belong to a different order (or rather disorder, *Unordnung*). The post-transformational years opened Poznań once again to Europe; moreover, "the laws of economy and social development" which replaced the communism system are perceived as natural in this city known for its long tradition of entrepreneurship and diligence. This "spirit of enterprise, renown for generations" (About the city 2012) is the driving force of the developmental discourse in contemporary Poznań.

To understand how it became a *spiritus movens* of the local politics, I will now shift the perspective and examine the ways in which transformations of the global capitalism affected the region and the city.

From Entrepreneurial Tradition to Entrepreneurial City

There is a vast amount of research on how global capital affects cities worldwide, and how their roles and positions changed when capitalism entered a new form, which Charles Sabel in the late 1980s called "flexibility" (Sabel 1989). A decade after Sabel, Bob Jessop noticed that "in contrast to the privileging of the national economy and national state in the period of Atlantic Fordism, no spatial scale is currently privileged. Instead there is a more complex nesting and weaving of different spatial scales.... This creates complex and changing opportunities for cities to organize territory as a place for production and for fixing capital in place and to organize the city as a space of flows to capture surpluses from the movement of capital and labour" (Jessop 2013 [1998]; cf. Hall and Hubbard 1998: 160). This need to "capture surpluses from the movement of capital" lies behind the after-transformational strategy in Poznań, and behind the decision to host Euro 2012.

In the reality where big companies act and are considered as if they were individuals (Harvey 2005), we can also observe a shift to a perspective which sees regions, not their inhabitants, as instrumental actors (Swyngedouw et al. 2002). Therefore, it is common to talk about regions as good or attractive ones, rather than about the needs of their inhabitants. It also justifies the shift in urban politics, which is now reoriented towards "regional success", i.e. towards attracting the flows of capital (Smith 1999: 144). State actors, region and city authorities work closely with business and this collaboration has a strong influence on regional and city governance (cf. Harvey 2005; Jessop 2013 [1998]). Smith also argues that "business institutions begin to spread into social institutions that had hitherto retained a certain distance and distinctiveness from them" (Smith 1999: 146–7). In an effort to attract capital and achieve the "regional success", cities practise marketing or urban branding. Harvey noticed in the late 1980s that "in recent years, urban governance has become increasingly preoccupied with the exploration of new ways in which to foster and encourage local development and employment growth. Such an entrepreneurial stance contrasts with the managerial practices of earlier decades which primarily focused on the local provision of services, facilities and benefits to urban populations" (Harvey 1989a: 3). The author of "A Brief History of Neoliberalism" traces the roots of the modern entrepreneurial discourse back to New York City in the early 1970s. For the investment bankers who started to decide about the city budgeting policies in what was the outcome of the fiscal crisis, "the creation of a 'good business climate' was a priority.... The city's elite institutions were mobilized to sell the image of the city as a cultural centre and tourist destination (inventing the famous logo 'I Love New York').... Artistic freedom and artistic license, promoted by the city's powerful cultural institutions, led, in effect, to the neoliberalization of culture.... New York became the epicenter of postmodern culture and intellectual experimentation. Meanwhile, the investment bankers reconstructed the city economy around financial activities, ancillary services such as legal services and the media (much revived by the financialization occurring), and diversified consumerism (gentrification and neighbourhood 'restoration' playing a prominent and profitable role). City government was more and more construed as an entrepreneurial rather than a social democratic or even managerial entity. Inter-urban competition for investment capital transformed government into urban governance through public-private partnership. City business was increasingly conducted behind closed doors, and the democratic and representational content of local governance diminished" (Harvey 2005: 47; cf. Swyngedouw et al. 2002). Glick Schiller and Çağlar also notice that after the age of heavy industry, today new cities require lifestyle facilities and an urban cultural profile (Glick Schiller and Çağlar 2011c: 72): these are the demands of the modern global economy. New economic conditions imply the growing significance of branding and city marketing, where "local culture" is used to increase the investment attractiveness of the locality. The regions and cities of today, as Glick Schiller and Çağlar stress: "are affected by global competition for investment, new-economy industries, and changing market pressures, including those that favour gentrification and urban recognition. These pressures lead city leaders and developers around the world to promote their city as a global 'brand'" (Glick Schiller and Çağlar 2011b: 2). Culture, therefore, is used to attract capital and increase local competitiveness.

Moreover, as Ayşe Çağlar argues, the "hierarchies and structural positioning of cities and localities (urban zones) in general are no longer simply nested in interstate or national-regional hierarchies, but are located differently depending on their positioning in relation to global, national and regional circuits of capital flows" (Çağlar 2010: 115). States continue to be important players in those processes and can boost the competitiveness of certain regions and cities, in the sense that they decide on subsidies and provision of key infrastructural facilities and public services (Glick Schiller and Çağlar 2011c: 72).

In sum, the competition in attracting global capital under new economic conditions gave rise to entrepreneurial cities (Çağlar 2010: 119; cf. Harvey 1989a; Hall and Hubbard 1998; Jessop 2013 [1997]; [1998]), whose objective is "the socio-economic development of the city rather than the provision of welfare services to the inhabitants of the city; thus they are growth oriented rather than concerned with the income redistribution" (Çağlar 2010: 119). The growth-oriented, entrepreneurial developmental strategies of modern cities have been discussed extensively in interdisciplinary scholarship. Bob Jessop problematized the rise of entrepreneurial city in his two articles from the late 1990s (2013 [1997]; 2013 [1998]), where he discussed urban policies in the United Kingdom. The geographer analysed the links between the local (promotional) discourses about the "entrepreneurial character" of the city and specific urban governance mechanisms which refer to these discourses, and how both are interconnected with the global capital flows on the one hand, and with the particular structural, institutional and historical context of locality on the other hand. This perspective allowed him to see the rise of entrepreneurial cities as a structural answer to the challenges which the West had faced in post-Fordist capitalism; and the promotional campaigns as constructed "narratives which have been persuasively (but not necessarily intentionally) combined to consolidate a limited but widely accepted set of diagnoses and prescriptions for economic and political difficulties" (Jessop 2013 [1997]). One of the key features of those regional narratives is their *selective use of historical moments and forces as the key points of reference in entrepreneurial cities' developmental strategies*; certain moments from the region's past are invoked in order to legitimize particular ways of governance and dealing with the current economic, social and political problems. Although Jessop's contribution refers to the conditions in Western Europe and North America in the second half of the last century, the entrepreneurial city is definitely not a concept constrained to this specific time and place.

Jessop insists on analysing the local entrepreneurial discourses and practices in relation to the particular setting. Their appeal, effectiveness and plausibility depend on "their links to wider cultural and institutional formations" (Jessop 2013 [1997]), and to both personal- and metanarratives. The stronger the city's entrepreneurial strategy is embedded in the local context, and the closer related it is to individual and metanarratives, the more natural and commonsensical it appears. Jessop argues that "being an 'entrepreneurial city' has become a central element in many cities' self-images and/or place marketing activities. Entrepreneurial cities promote their preferable economic conditions for investment and as such market themselves as 'business-friendly'" (Jessop 2013 [1998]). To appear as such, they selectively chose some elements from their history and build on them a persuasive (effective, appealing, plausible and embedded in those past events and therefore "natural") promotional discourse of an entrepreneurial city. Both in the British cases described by Jessop and in that of Poznań, official rhetoric selectively draws on the past: communism is not used as a positive point of reference in the official "branding" strategy, whereas interwar Poznań is referred to as the land of milk and honey.

Interestingly, Jessop points out that many regions and cities focus solely on promotional campaigns and pay little attention to establishing governance mechanisms which would allow them to become truly entrepreneurial. He argues that the pro-business official discourse is seldom coupled with a genuine change in urban policies. Only few cities systematically and systemically work on increasing their competitiveness through institutional innovativeness and enhanced productivity, whereas in most cases urban activities are limited to multiplying "[c]onsultants' reports, outline proposals, non-binding agreements, glossy brochures, more or less regular conferences, meetings, or seminars, cultural exchanges, data bases, and information centres, (...) small-scale partnerships with limited coordination, insufficient resources, and often conflicting goals, (...) civic boosterism and deregulatory place-marketing" Jessop (1998 [2013]). This is not enough to consolidate and increase the city's competitiveness.[6]

Most of the strategies implemented by cities create so-called weaker forms of competition (Jessop 1998 [2013]), which are not focused on innovation, but targeted only at capturing inward investment from mobile capital. Two of them appear particularly relevant for my argument. In the "resource procurement" model, the authorities, facing a lack of certain resources – be they financial, territorial or human – are determined to access assets from the state or the EU (especially through structural funds). Accessing them usually requires adjusting local development plans and strategies in response to particular constraints and delimits the range of initiatives which can be pursued. The authorities must therefore decide between an independent development path and limited resources on the one hand, and a limited autonomy and significant resources on the other. Jessop notes that initiatives aimed at advancing the prestige and attractiveness of the city may have very little significance for the well-being of its inhabitants; in this model, "economic development strategies tend to result in jobs for commuters and entertainment for the suburban middle class", and can therefore threaten the legitimacy of the system. In the "place marketing" model, the focal point of urban policies is image construction and promotional activities, usually taking the form of reconstructing and reinventing local traditions. Although this can attract investment, it is usually limited to a few flagship projects which are not based in any long-term development strategy. In the entrepreneurial strategy in Poznań, hardly concerned with broad structural changes and innovations (which would enhance the city's long-term competitiveness), the biggest emphasis has been placed on promotional discourse. This "weaker form of competition strategy" in Poznań is determined to attract resources from the EU and to organize flagship projects. The leitmotif of this discourse has been the idiom of "metropolis", which represents an urban dream of becoming a

---

[6] It deserves to be emphasized here that Jessop, although analysing the strengths and weaknesses of urban entrepreneurial strategies, is eager to search for alternative solutions to this model of modernization.

truly Western, competitive city. An example of such rhetoric was the extract from the city's web page quoted at the beginning of this chapter.

As we have seen, in the common knowledge confirmed by Stryjakiewicz and others, Poznań entered the global competition for capital later than western cities, as a result of Poland's economic and political transformation in 1989. The course of the events which led to this moment is not the main subject of this dissertation and, unfortunately, it cannot be discussed here in length. There are several illuminating anthropological books and articles on the ways in which capitalism was reintroduced in East and Central Europe, including Poland (e.g. Wedel 1992, 2001; Dunn 2004; Buchowski 2001, 2006; Buchowski et al. 2001; Hann 1980; Hann et al. 2005; Humphrey 1983; Schneider 2012; Conte and Giordano 1999; Stacul 2014). I am deliberately talking about the reintroduction rather than introduction of capitalism in the region: I agree with Carol Nagengast when she says that "the reinstitution of capitalism in Poland was not the logical and inevitable victory of a superior system but rather... this new, old capitalism also reflects processes set into motion in the eighteen, nineteenth, and early twentieth centuries" (Nagengast 1991: 1). Many of those accounts point to the neoliberal character of those changes (cf. Ost 2005; Lipton and Sachs 1990). Harvey shows that the indebted countries of Central and East Europe were forced to implement neoliberal institutional reforms in order to have their debt payment rescheduled or cancelled. This "structural adjustment" was a requirement of the IMF and World Bank, which "became centres for the propagation and enforcement of 'free market fundamentalism' and neoliberal orthodoxy" (Harvey 2005: 29). However, neo-liberalism is one of those broad concepts which are seldom defined in literature, almost a "dustbin category" (Sayer and Walker 1992: 177–8) for encompassing all, often contradictory, processes associated with the late capitalism (although Harvey himself is one of those authors who deliver an extensive definition of the term). James Ferguson cogently discusses the negative consequences of the uses, misuses and abuses of the term (Ferguson 2010). I am not so much interested in labelling the processes which took place in Poland in late 1980s and 1990s, as in observing how the "reinstitution of capitalism" was actually achieved; in other words, how the trajectories of post-transformational processes were linked with the city's past through what might be called "mythopraxis" (Sahlins 1985).

The future shape and standards of Polish economic politics for the next decades was determined by the "shock therapy". It was implemented by professor Leszek Balcerowicz, the former chair of the National Bank of Poland and Deputy Prime Minister in the first non-communist government of Tadeusz Mazowiecki. This economic transformation programme is commonly referred to as "the Balcerowicz Plan". Although his politics and views have been widely criticized, he remains a determined advocate of the free market. Witold Gadomski, a renowned publicist at "Gazeta Wyborcza" and for years an adherent of the free market, wrote in 2013 that almost 25 years after the transformation, "Poland is still ruled by Balcerowicz" (Gadomski 2013). The rhetoric of the free market and privatization remained hegemonic in the Polish political debate for years and determined people's individual choices and strategies. Only the failure of the Civic Platform in the May 2015 presidential election and in the October 2015 parliamentary election proved that this hegemony was eventually questioned.

But back in 2014, Sławomir Sierakowski, a publicist and an editor-in-chief of the leftist "Krytyka Polityczna", pointed out that "for the last 20 years people have been told that democracy equals human rights plus a free market without any social commitments. And they have learned it" (Sierakowski 2014: 27). The philosopher and historian of ideas Andrzej Walicki wrote about the "bad luck" of the Polish reformers:

[They] wanted to replace the People's Republic of Poland's planned economy with a "normal" market economy, [but] their activity coincided with the neoliberal right-wing' offensive, which pretended to be a consequent liberalism, whereas in fact it was deeply hostile to the hitherto direction of the development of liberal societies. (Walicki 2013b: 30)

He argued that "[although] luckily, Poland did not became a neoliberal orthodoxy (...), neoliberalism has become the dominant ideology for the considerable part of the political class and for the media (...) [who are] the beneficiaries of the system". Marcin Król, a philosopher, publicist and in the 1980s an oppositionist, seemed to confirm this view when he criticized the Polish transformation in the interview (which was part of a series published in Gazeta Wyborcza in 2013 and 2014 and conducted by a left-wing journalist, Grzegorz Sroczyński):

> We were stupid. In the 80s we were infected by the neoliberal ideology and I am personally responsible for that too: I was persuading Tusk and Bielecki, the whole Gdańsk circle. I gave them Hayek to read. I had similar views to Balcerowicz, but today the two of us see things differently (...) We all believed in a certain fiction, inherited, by the way, from resistance literature. The fiction of the free market. A bookish one. The two most important books of that time were Hayek's "Free market and freedom" and Popper's "Open society". (...) [They shaped our] belief that a free man will always find a place for himself, that the free market will absorb any number of employees, and all you have to do is set it in motion. (...). (Król 2014: 12–14)

David Ost, a historian and author of several books on Polish transformation, argued that in 1989, Poland essentially had no other choice:

> You have to have a look at what Poles did differently from what they wanted in 1980. Solidarity in 1980 was not fighting for capitalism for sure. (...) The West in the 80s changed a lot. When [Solidarity] was born, the world and Europe were still ruled by social democracy. Its time was coming to an end, but Thatcher had only recently won the election and there was no "Washington consensus" yet, no list of the rules for the neoliberal modifications of the economy (...). Therefore I cannot agree... that in 1989 Poland had a free choice of what kind of capitalism it wanted to have. The field of choice was in the 70s. In the 80s globalization was already happening. (...) Thanks to globalization, capitalists could break the alliance with their workers. They started to pay less and reduced the social/welfare legislation. Of course, there were some social-democratic models of capitalism, for instance in Scandinavia, but back then they were undergoing crisis. Moreover, Poles were looking at the market economy from the perspective of real socialism. They wrote very little about Western European systems: the ideal was America. (Ost 2014: 32; cf. Sierakowski 2014: 27)

But many "stars" of the transformation have become more critical about the course which the transition took in Poland. Jan Krzysztof Bielecki, the former Prime Minister and the chair of Pekao Bank, recalls

> We tried to think like Hayek (*myśleć Hayekiem*), or like Friedman. . . . In 1989 that was my way of thinking: there is too much state, it smothers us, enslaves us, we lack freedom and personal property. Therefore, if we want to change the world, we have to be more Hayek-like than Hayek. (Bielecki 2014: 14)

The famous oppositionist Karol Modzelewski recalled that in the late 1980s and at the beginning of the 1990s everyone talked about "building capitalism" in Poland and hardly anyone noticed that it was a calque of the term used in the previous system: "building socialism" (Modzelewski 2013: 14).

The implementation of the "neoliberal logic" in Poland, as depicted by the critics above, was very much dependent on the semi-peripheral position of the country. In OECD terminology, Poland is one of the "converging countries", which refers to the decrease in the distance from the economic development of the western countries, measured with indices of GDP per capita: from about 1/3 of the EU average at the beginning of transformation to the present 2/3 in the enlarged Union (Jasiecki 2013: 483). Elsewhere, GDP per capita was estimated at 10,000 dollars in 1989, and in 2012, at 21,500 dollars, which is 66% of the GDP in the EU (Gadomski 2013). In this hegemonic narrative, Poland is forced to "catch up" with the West. This is what David Ost had in mind when writing that "Poland had no choice in 1989", and this is what David Harvey emphasized when discussing the structural adjustment of the region. After years of enforced "Polish–Soviet friendship", Poland, like most countries from the former Eastern bloc, was determined to re-establish its business and political relations with the West and position itself against the East. For years, it was a strong drive behind strategic decisions of the state, also at the expense of economic self-containment. In his book on capitalism in Poland, Krzysztof Jasiecki (Jasiecki 2013) sees Poland as "occupying a subordinate, peripheral place in the global division of labour", which "even though a member of the

EU, remains a country of low institutional standards subordinating its development policy to the decisions of the main net contributors to the Union's budget (structural funds)" (485). As a result of the global transformations and due to the semi-peripheral position of Poland, the Polish economy, like other post-socialist states and relatively new EU members, tends to be more dependent on foreign capitalism than western European countries (Jasiecki 2013: 228–9, 289–309; cf. Orenstein 2014). Jasiecki points to the risks and systemic limitations of the Central-European scenario of economic development based on the leading role of foreign capitalism. The 2008 financial crisis exposed the costs and dangers of, as he calls it, the "peripheral integration" of the post-socialist states with the EU and global economy, which rely on foreign capital and exports to the European markets, and as such are very sensitive to market fluctuations (293).

The Poland's shifting attitude towards Ukraine illustrates how fluctuating and relational are the processes of "Othering" (cf. Baumann 2005). During Euro 2012, the co-host of the tournament was often "used" in the official rhetoric to present Poland as a democratic, modern and truly European country (cf. Kiel 2014). Two German authors in an article published in *Der Spiegel* a month before the football tournament wrote about the Polish–Ukrainian border:

> Sometimes you get an impression that from before the year when Poland entered the EU and Schengen Agreement the former Polish-German border moved 600 kilometers to the east. The same markets on the roadside, the same smuggling of cigarettes and alcohol. Simultaneously, also the slightly arrogant attitude towards the Eastern neighbour has moved. Ukraine has become for the Poles what Poland used to be for the Germans. (Follath and Puhl 2012: 9)

Poznań's standing and competitiveness strategy is particularly dependent on the opposition between the West and the East. The former is the synonym of the city's past and future ambitions. The latter of its (Slavic) "other" and the devalued period of the city's history under the (Eastern) communism. As I tried to show earlier, the city's branding, both international and within the state, is built on this crucial opposition. This is how Katarzyna Parysek, the head of the Fan Zone in Poznań during the Euro, described the citizens of Poznań a few days before the first whistle in a short interview given to the local newspaper:

> We are punctual and reliable, have a strong attention to detail and manage money well, and it is not true that we lack imagination. I appreciate our way of work, of doing things, and *I miss it when I am forced to work with people from the east bank of the Vistula river.* (Suchecka 2012: 12)

This processual positioning towards and against the East and the West; within the state, and in relation to the two capitals, Berlin and Warsaw; and against the flows of the global capital – all of them backed the narrative in which Euro 2012 was the jewel in the crown of Poznań's entrepreneurial strategy, presented as "embedded" (Polanyi 2001 [1944]) in the local traditions and mythopraxis.[7]

Having introduced a new territorial division in 1999, Poland has a three-tier administrative system, embracing the local level (*gmina*, commune, 2,486 in total), the supralocal or subregional level (*powiat*, 373 in total) and the regional level (*województwo*, voivodeship, 16 in total). Poznań is a municipal commune, and a capital of both the *powiat* and the Greater Poland voivodeship. It is the fifth largest city in Poland with roughly 600,000 inhabitants, and with the metropolitan region population (Poznań Metropolitan Region) of 850,000. It is ethnically homogeneous, yet lively thanks to its academic character (214 students per 1,000 inhabitants makes it first among the largest cities in the country), but also undergoing a process of fast suburbanization. According to a

---

[7] This discussion brings to mind the postcolonial strand of the social critique. The case of Poland and the postcommunist Eastern Europe in general can be analysed from the postcolonial perspective, see for instance: S. Chari and K. Verdery (2009) "Thinking Between the Posts: Postcolonialism, Postsocialism, and Ethnography After the Cold War" In: *Comparative Studies in Society and History* 51, 1, 6–34; H. Cervinkova (2012) "Postcolonialism, Postsocialism and the Anthropology of East-central Europe" In: *Journal of Postcolonial Writing*, 48, 2, 155–63; O. Obad (2008) "The European Union from the Postcolonial Perspective: Can the Periphery Ever Approach the Center?" In: *Stud. Ethnol. Croat.*, vol. 20, str. 9–35. One can be even tempted to refer to Michael Herzfeld's term of "crypto-colonialism", see: M. Herzfeld (2002) "The Absent Presence: Discourses of Crypto-Colonialism" In: *The South Atlantic Quarterly* 101, 4, 899–926; but elaboration on the subject is beyond the scope of this book.

CATI (computer-assisted telephone interviewing) survey conducted by Millward Brown SA, the number of citizens in Poznań drops every year. According to the Central Statistical Office of Poland (GUS), it will be lower than 500,000 in a few years (Lipoński 2013a: 1; cf. Stryjakiewicz et al. 2007: 1). In a centralized political and economic system which favours Warsaw as the focal political and economic centre in the country, for years now Poznań has been struggling to regain the title of Poland's second city. This struggle is fuelled by the process of creating the image of Poznań as a City of Work and Play, but first and foremost – as an entrepreneurial metropolis.

To this end, The New Strategy of the Poznań City Brand Name was launched in the spring of 2009 and enumerated several companies which were presented as the "business cards of the know-how city". The city promotional campaign "Poznan* the city of know-how" was devised to attract new investors and capital to the city, and as such it could be seen as an unequivocal expression of Poznań's new entrepreneurial promotional strategy. The marketing strategy was designed by a consortium consisting of the advertising agency Just and the Institute for the Competitive Economy of Regions for 2.9 million zloties (about 200,000 euro), while its implementation cost about 25–30 million zloties (6–7.5 million euro). These amounts were fiercely criticized by public opinion as just a façade (for more on the discussion of the launch of the strategy, see: Stryjakiewicz et al. 2010: 52–3). Since its launch, the slogan has often been used ironically by the mayor's critics, also during my research. This critique is in line with what Bob Jessop stressed when he insisted that urban entrepreneurial activities cannot be reduced merely to economic activities, nor to a city's promotional campaign aiming to present it as an entrepreneurial locality. It was noticed by the citizens who saw the inconsistency between the city's promotional campaign and sociopolitical praxis.

The question whether Poznań can be perceived as a metropolis preoccupied people's minds in the times when the 1964 survey discussed above was conducted, and in its aftermath, when it was interpreted in 1984 (Znaniecki and Ziółkowski 1984). Metropolitan character, Ziółkowski explained elsewhere (Ziółkowski 1967), refers to particular social features and ways of behaving, and not every big city can be called a metropolis. On the contrary, even a relatively small town can be called metropolitan on the basis of social and cultural criteria; but a city cannot be called a metropolis if it is not metropolitan (Znaniecki and Ziółkowski 1984: 214). Metropolitan, according to the authors, equals heterogeneity; a cultural pluralism of essences and incentives; a national and supernatural influence; and an ability to create new social and cultural standards; in brief, it means everything but parochialism. Ziółkowski argues that with its passive elites, hermetic scientific environment and without a modern, metropolitan city centre, Poznań is a typical provincial capital (Ziółkowski 1967: 13).

Although Poznań was considered a big city in 1964, it was commonly described by the respondents as non-metropolitan: they saw it as "big, but not metropolitan" (Znaniecki and Ziółkowski 1984: 214). The sociologists summarized the results and listed the main flaws of the non-metropolitan Poznań: "there is no city centre, little street life, the city is empty at night . . . it lacks metropolitan or city characteristics . . . a provincial style of life is stressed . . . [as well as] torpor of the elites (. . .). There is also severe criticism of the city's cultural facilities and institutions" (Znaniecki and Ziółkowski 1984: 217). The respondents were aware of the fact that although the city could have scientific or cultural institutions of metropolitan character and perform multiply economic and sociocultural functions – i.e. be metropolitan in a formal sense – it did not necessarily mean that it possessed the qualitative features which would have made it metropolitan. "It is not only form, but also substance that matters", aptly concluded one of the citizens quoted by the authors (Znaniecki and Ziółkowski 1984: 214).

Like the impression shared by many contemporary citizens concerned about the urban chaos and processes of suburbanization (cf. Stryjakiewicz et al. 2007), in 1964 some respondents noticed that too much construction was taking place in the suburbs and on the outskirts of Poznań, whereas the city centre remained neglected. One of the respondents compared the city to a "pretzel" (*obwarzanek*) (1968 survey: generation II, Znaniecki and Ziółkowski 1984: 238), and another to a "beautiful woman without teeth" (1968 survey: generation II, Znaniecki and Ziółkowski 1984: 238). The respondents criticized the lack of urban planning, bad condition of housing and poor shape of the city's green areas (262–74); as one of them argued: "It is difficult to call Poznan a modern city. It would have been such, if right after regaining independence in 1919 a specialist had sat down and worked on the urban planning. But no, we just started to build new buildings on the peripheries and did not think about the city centre" (1964 survey: generation I, Znaniecki and Ziółkowski 1984: 227). One answer is particularly striking when compared to today's discussion on whether a steady and planned development in Poland is possible at all: "I have an impression that in our city most investments depend on times of prosperity, and money is found for new developments only when it is related to the International Fair" (1968 survey: generation II, Znaniecki and Ziółkowski 1984: 248).

However, at the time of my research, Poznań's authorities' ambition was to present the city as a bustling metropolis: the City of Work and Play (About the city 2012). Becoming a recognizable metropolis is one of the four strategic goals in Poznań's most important official documents (Strategia 2030 2013: 86). The City Strategy differentiates between two definitions of metropolis: in one, the term is used interchangeably with "agglomeration" and refers to the geographical position of Poznań as a suburbanized economic and cultural centre; in the other, metropolis is a prestigious rank acknowledging the city's high international standing as a competitive and attractive location. Geographers who tried to estimate the creative potential of the city (Stryjakiewicz et al. 2007, 2010), although aware of the factual position of Poznań,[8] eagerly used the term in their discussion on its future development: by doing so, they confirmed the importance of this aspiration for the city's "branding".

---

[8] They define Poznań metropolitan region as "located within the so-called Central European banana, i.e. an area of accelerated growth. In relation to the whole of Europe, however, the growth potential of Polish cities (including Poznań) is rather small. In a report on the European Regional Economic Growth Index (EREGI) published by Jones Lang LaSalle in October 2006 and embracing 91 big cities of Europe, Poznań took 52nd place (after Warsaw, 44th, but before other Polish cities: Cracow 71st, Wroclaw 74th, Katowice 81st, Gdansk-Gdynia-Sopot 83rd, Lodz 84th, Szczecin 89th). What is worth noting, however, is the fact that among the cities of post-communist East-Central Europe Poznań was ranked sixth, recording the steepest growth in this group: in comparison with the year 2005 it had moved up by as many as 24 places (while Warsaw dropped by 23 places). The report emphasises that Poznań is not only one of the fastest- but also most evenly-growing Polish metropolises" (Stryjakiewicz et al. 2007: 23).

This association between metropolis and entrepreneurial development was also obvious in my conversations with civil servants in the Town Hall. When I asked them what kind of city Poznań would be in 2030, they imagined it as a recognizable and business-friendly, as an economic and business centre – and in sum, as a European metropolis. This vision was embedded in their understanding of the local *genius loci*:

This is our five minutes after Warsaw, Cracow and Wrocław. We are distinguished by our work ethic, we are business-minded and entrepreneurial, and hence our motto, Eastern Energy, Western Style, western standards of life and work and eastern creativity and imagination. I think that is why we stand out from a crowd.

3

"Like Pharaoh, Like Pyramid". Embedding Sports Mega-Event in the Local Tradition

The majority of the research on urban development projects (UDPs) is focused on presenting a broad, theoretical perspective on changing urban policies and the role of megaprojects in it, sometimes drawing conclusions from comparative analysis of several case studies. It usually uses quantitative methods (the Vancouver-based study of M.D. Lowes [2002] is one great exception here); and until recently predominantly discussed examples from the post-Fordist and post-Keynesian Western European setting (although this has changed on account of mega-events in Brazil, Sochi and Qatar). This endeavour is first and foremost interested in discussing the embeddedness of the mega-event in the local *knowledge* and modernization processes. Euro 2012 was hosted by former Eastern bloc countries and as such it must be analysed in terms of the very particular historical and geopolitical context. However, this study must also be positioned against the current state of the art.

Megaprojects, including mega-events, have been extensively studied, mostly by geographers and social scientists. They are seen as both expressions of the neo-liberal hegemonic ideology and as an "integral part of urban re-imaging strategies" (Hall 2006: 63), as they derive from

© The Author(s) 2017
M.Z. Kowalska, *Urban Politics of a Sporting Mega Event*,
Football Research in an Enlarged Europe,
DOI 10.1007/978-3-319-52105-3_3

and at the same time transform the local policy and governmentality. Geographers Swyngedouw, Moulaert and Rodriguez (2002) argue that large-scale UDPs, including sports mega-events, are probably the most visible outcomes of the New Economic Policy (NEP) on an urban scale, which they call a New Urban Policy (NUP). They compared studies of 13 large-scale European UDPs and concluded that they are both "*part* of a neo-liberal NUP approach and its selective 'middle- and upper-class' democracy" and *tools* for establishing new forms of planning and governing, "characterized by less democratic and more elite-driven priorities" (Swyngedouw et al. 2002: 542). NUP aims at changing regions into attractive locations for business and leisure. UDPs are the outcome of such policy, and simultaneously they serve as stimulus for its further development.

Moreover, if cities today exemplify the fusion of entrepreneurialism and neo-liberalism, and dominance of competitiveness hegemony with their narrow elitist interests (as discussed in the previous chapter), megaprojects are seen as excellent instruments to accumulate capital and gain advantage in the global economy (Hall 2006: 64–7). Geographers note that megaprojects and mega-events are "emblematic examples of neo-liberal forms of urban governance . . . [and] embody and express processes that reflect global pressures and incorporate changing systems of local, regional, and/or national regulation and governance" (Swyngedouw et al. 2002: 543). New urban strategies are local answers produced to meet the requirements of the global economic system. UDPs express the logic pursued by city elites, which aims at enhancing local competitiveness and urban growth through place-marketing and attracting investment capital. As such, "urban projects . . . are . . . not the mere result, response, or consequence of political and economic change choreographed elsewhere. On the contrary . . . UDPs are the very catalysts of urban and political change, fuelling processes that are felt not only locally, but regionally, nationally, and internationally as well. It is such concrete interventions that express and shape transformations in spatial political and economic configurations. They illustrate the actual concrete process through which postmodern forms, post-Fordist economic dynamics, and neoliberal systems of governance are crafted and through which a new articulation of regulatory and governmental scales is produced. UDPs are productive of and embody processes that operate in and over a variety of scales, from the local to the regional, the national, the European, and the global scale" (Swyngedouw et al. 2002: 546). To conclude, megaprojects, including mega-events, can be seen as both hallmarks and strategic instruments of the urban politics, which (1) derive from the preconditions of the global economy, (2) enable rent accumulation through redirecting public resources to certain type of investments and (3) change the governing procedures in the name of economic growth and benefits to the whole community due to the international promotion of the hosting city (cf. Hall 2006; Swyngedouw et al. 2002).

Although the geographers' analysis pertains to Western, post-Fordist (and post-Keynesian) systems at the beginning of the century, in socio-economic regulation in Polish cities we can observe the same "gradual shift away from distributive policies, welfare considerations, and direct service provision towards more market-oriented and market-dependent approaches aimed at pursuing economic promotion and competitive restructuring" (Swyngedouw et al. 2002: 548). In most cities, as the authors note and as also occurred in the Polish host cities for Euro 2012, landmark events and other urban revitalization projects are presented as necessary preconditions for economic growth. Such projects usually unite different political and lobby groups and change local policy into even more entrepreneurially oriented (548). Flagship projects as expressions and catalysts of new urban priorities. With their new urban coalitions, shift from social to economic policy, new state entrepreneurialism, selective deregulation, city marketing, territorially targeted social policy and production of urban rent (Swyngedouw et al. 2002: 548), they lead to the polarization of society: large urban projects are associated with the interests of particular social groups and with the exclusion of others. New urban governance is project-oriented (565–6) and "circumvent, bypass, ignore, or marginalize certain social groups" (566). It forms new authoritarian coalitions, which "create a public discourse on the importance of the project and define it as a particular milestone in the shaping of the future of the city, and their interventions are presented as essential to maintaining a viable position in the interurban competition" (566). Flyvbjerg

(2013) notices great enthusiasm among politicians who "love building monuments to themselves and their causes" (28), as well as among business people looking forward to making money on new investments. He enumerates the beneficiaries of the projects: "contractors, engineers, architects, consultants, construction and transportation workers, bankers, investors, landowners, lawyers, and developers lap up the rewards, while the financial risks frequently fall on the taxpayer" (Flyvbjerg 2013: 28). Despite this unequal share of benefits, not that difficult to foresee, megaprojects are sold to the public on the grounds of job creation, economic gains, better public services, infrastructural improvements and public good. As a result, public funds (including EU funding) are not redistributed on the basis of universal social needs but are allocated on a project-formulation basis and as such serve an elitist social configuration (Swyngedouw et al. 2002: 565). The socioeconomic restricting of modern cities leads to the creation of urban "islands of wealth" (567) and "patchwork spaces" (571).

Swyngedouw and other geographers put emphasis on the formalist application of local democratic mechanisms and little if any public consultations at the stage of initiation of UDPs. They argue that "although a varying choreography of state, private sector, and nongovernmental organization participation is usually present... these forms of urban governance show a significant deficit with respect to accountability, representation, and the presence of formal rules of inclusion or participation. Indeed, accountability channels are often gray, nonformalized, and nontransparent, frequently circumventing traditional democratic channels of accountability" (556; 561). As such, they express the demands, needs and aspiration of only those included in this new type of governing, who gain a great degree of autonomy and are able to avoid public debate over possible (alternative) solutions. The examples from Poznań show it could be done on the grounds of commercial or legal confidentiality, but also through disregarding the opposing views and critique as irrational or based on uneconomic, "political" (i.e. personal), and therefore false premises, as I will discuss below.

As policy and politics meet the needs of those who have a pivotal role in planning, organizing or implementing UDPs, the very projects can illustrate the temporary results and shapes of power struggles in a given setting. They can be called, according to Swyngedouw et al., "'elite playing fields', on which the stake is to shape an urban future in line with the aspirations of the most powerful segment(s) among the participants" at a given time (Swyngedouw et al. 2002: 563). Megaprojects and mega-events are therefore lenses which enable us to observe negotiations between different powers and visions in a given location and the changeable outcome of those struggles.

The Event

Before Euro 2012, both the national and local media celebrated Poland's victorious bid and presented the key investments which the host cities planned to complete before the Championship. In November 2007, "Głos Wielkopolski", one of the two major dailies in Poznań, published a list of such key projects planned in the city under the title "Euro 2012 will turn Poznań into the city of dreams" (Rembowski 2007). With the cost of renovating the city stadium estimated at 400 million zloties (or 100 million euro) and partly financed by the EU, and with many long-awaited investment projects in transportation, and the sports and cultural infrastructure, in retrospect all this proved to be nothing more than just a wishful thinking. The article listed 20 major projects whose completion was either estimated at a much lower cost than required (and often did not qualify for financial support from European funds, as in the case of the stadium, where the renovation costs had to be covered almost solely by the city), or never actually started (as in the case of modernizing the Arena events hall, of sports venues in Golęcin and Chwiałka, and certain road projects); several minor investments were also mentioned by the author and supplemented by a short interview with the then vice-mayor of the city, Maciej Frankiewicz, a leading ambassador of the event. All projects were supposed to be completed before 2012.

Euro 2012 was different from the UDPs and mega-events described by geographers in this respect in that it was the local government, not the national one which bore a major share of the costs and risks of hosting the event in the city (Whitson and Horne 2006: 78;

Swyngedouw et al. 2002: 551–6). Despite initial hopes in Poznań, it appeared that neither the state government nor the EU was willing to provide financial support for certain investments which the municipality considered crucial, such as the city stadium, or the so-called third frame, a transport route described by Poznań City Hall as essential for the city's development (Nawrot 2008).

The old city stadium at Bułgarska Street was chosen as Poznań's Euro venue. It was opened in 1980 and since then has been used by the local *Ekstraklasa*[1] football club, which moved here from the old grounds in Dębiec. The modernization of the stadium began in 2003 when a new fourth stand was erected to close the characteristic horseshoe shape of the other three stands. This initial revamp of the historical venue transmuted into a new project, and the fourth stand was complemented by three new stands, all covered with a light membrane. The four stands differ in size (three of them are three-tiered, one has two tiers), which results in the asymmetrical shape of the ground. The seating capacity is 43,269, which slightly exceeds the UEFA-set minimum capacity for a European Championship venue (cf. Stadion Lecha 2012, Stadion miejski w Poznaniu 2012). The official opening of the stadium featuring a concert by Sting took place on the 20th September 2010, making it the first Polish venue opened for the Euro. During the tournament in 2012, three matches were played at the stadium: on the 10th of June between Ireland and Croatia, on the 14th between Italy and Croatia and on the 18th between Ireland and Italy.

The modernization was initially estimated at approximately 436 million zloties but was granted roughly 110 million zloties (30 million euros) from the state, just 30% of the required outlay. In 2008, the local government already knew that it could not count on any European funds being used for the modernization: Portugal, the host of the previous Championship, had to return the money it spent on building two of its Euro Championship stadiums to the European Commission

---

[1] The Ekstraklasa is the Poland's top professional league for association football clubs, comprising 16 clubs (ekstraklasa.net), including *Kolejowy Klub Sportowy*, KKS Lech Poznań, traditionally known also as *Kolejorz* (meaning a "railwayman" in the local dialect).

and experienced serious problems with maintaining the venues (Wilczak 2012). Eventually, the Polish government paid only 15% of the 750 million zloties total cost of the stadium: the rest had to be covered by the city (cf. Marecki 2011; Kokot and Karbowiak 2012). The cost of the stadiums built for Euro 2012 amounts to 4.5 billion zloties. The costs of the venues reached nearly 2 billion zloties in Warsaw and around 850 zloties in Wrocław and Gdańsk; the reserve-venues in Cracow and Chorzów cost almost 600 million zloties each (construction in Chorzów is still far from completion) (Stadiony 2012; cf. Bujalski, Wesołowski, Karendys 2012, Wojtczuk 2012).

Various studies point to the "performance paradox of megaprojects" (Flyvbjerg, Bruzelius and Rothengatter 2003) or the "governance paradox" (Arena and Molloy 2010) and the escalation of mega-investments' planned costs. Scholars generally agree that megaprojects are always risky, and that their success depends on rent returns (Swyngedouw et al. 2002: 566–7). Flyvbjerg (2014: 9; cf. Flyvbjerg 2017) talks about the "iron law of megaprojects: over budget, over time, over and over again", whereas Horne and Manzenreiter (2006: 10) prove that sports mega-events are the outcomes of the "fantasy world of underestimated costs, overestimated revenues, underestimated environmental impacts and over-valued economic development effects". Sinking money and investment into certain type of projects and infrastructure may potentially bring benefits, but, as Swyngedouw et al. point out, those benefits "are almost always reaped by the private sector" (2002: 556). Meanwhile, the cost of "white elephants", whose costly maintenance is out of proportion to their usefulness, is borne by taxpayers, who are the usual sponsors of the sporting venues.

The final cost of the city stadium in Poznań grew significantly from the first estimates. The pitch had to be replaced six times during the first year of operation, some parts of the stadium were flooded several times during heavy rainfall, and some major construction faults were discovered after the opening of the stadium (cf. Kierownik budowy kłamał 2014). Janusz Rajewski, the former chair of POSiR (*Poznańskie Ośrodki Sportu i Rekreacji*, the municipal company responsible for sports venues), apparently forgot to include a paragraph about copyright in the agreement with the architect of the stadium. Consequently, the city had to pay extra for all amendments to the stadium, and was eventually forced to buy the copyright for 2 million zloties (Grobelny 2014). Although a survey conducted right after the event showed that its approval rating was almost 100% (Euro 2012, nr 2), the profit and loss account was soon subjected to critical scrutiny.

The official sources announced that the profits from hosting the event amounted to 242,094,411.24 zloties, but this figure includes Advertising Value Equivalency (AVE) estimated at 231,000,000 (231 million zloties, including 130 in international media), i.e. almost the total of the claimed public benefit of the tournament (Euro 2012, nr 2). AVE is the amount of money which would have to be paid for editorial, Internet, radio or TV coverage if it was an advertisement. This index is used to measure PR efficiency, although today even within the PR sector worldwide, it is heavily criticized as misleading and dubious. The direct costs of the event were estimated at 20,493,530.91 zloties (Euro 2012, nr 2). The costs of the official Fan Zone built in the city centre amounted to 9,341,929 zloties (Euro 2012, nr 2). Apart from the Fan Zone, the rest was spent on necessary facilities and management of the event: public transportation, additional parking spaces, cleaning, decorations, additional Fan Zone etc. Other sources (Deloitte 2012) say that Poznań spent 24.8 million zloties (roughly 6 million euro) on the preparation and promotion of the event. These figures, however, do not include the costs of the stadium and loans taken out for Poznań's own contribution to infrastructural projects funded by the EU, which together proved to be a great burden on the public purse. Moreover, as other scholars point out (Woźniak 2013), reports estimating benefits of the tournament were usually commissioned and/or produced by the same institutions which were highly interested in hosting the event (and indeed made a profit), and as such were biased and far-fetched. Of course, one might say that such spending was justified and beneficial to the city, but, as experts argue, the EU funds aimed at stimulating innovation and development were instead "concreted" in buildings and roads (Kozak 2015).

With each year, the annual city budgets became more and more problematic, both due to the pro-investment strategy of the city, which decided to maximize the use of EU funding, and to some crucial changes in the fiscal law on the state level. The fiscal changes introduced in Poland in 2007–2009 (especially the lowering of Personal Income Taxes, introduction of family tax relief) and the change in financing the education system (since 2013, the growing proportion of expenditure on education has to be paid by local governments) are unfavourable to urban budgets. Furthermore, the city is obliged to pay compensation to investors (developers) whose projects could not be built due to changes in the land-use planning (50 million zloties in 2012, the Euro year). Poland's local governments (*samorządy*) are undergoing a serious crisis of financial autonomy. State subsidies do not cover all local expenses, revenues are falling, and investment is highly dependent on EU funding. Discussing those changes is beyond the scope of this book, but it must be emphasized that they all determine the financial condition of the city. Under these circumstances, hosting Euro 2012 was a luxury which the local government, as I argue, simply could not afford. In 2010, the city's debt was estimated at 1.6 billion zloties (Kisiel 2009); four years after the tournament its debt amounted to 1.8 billion zloties, i.e. c. 420 million euro (Wieloletnia prognoza finansowa miasta 2016). Although the city's debt has exceeded the maximum limit of 59.9% of budget income and already in 2013 amounted to 75% (Fitch potwierdził ratingi 2014), mayor Ryszard Grobelny argued that also the legendary interwar mayor Cyryl Ratajski had indebted the city when organizing the General Exhibition in 1929. Ratajski was then rescued by a government act, which cancelled the city's debt. It seems that this time around the city authorities also placed their trust in central government.

Before the tournament, politicians declared that the stadiums would be used as concert venues. Rafał Dutkiewicz, the mayor of Wrocław, proudly emphasized the multifunctional character of the city stadium during its official opening: "Besides matches, we will organize big music concerts, and there will be place for offices, concert halls, and restaurants. This is something that we dreamt of" (Kokot and Karbowiak 2012). Despite those promises, it transpired that the Euro stadiums are best suited to football matches, and little else. Not only did the few concerts organized in Poznań and elsewhere in Poland turn out to be unprofitable, they were also costly. Wrocław had to pay more than 5 million zloties extra for a

George Michael concert and the boxing match between Vitali Klitschko and Tomasz Adamek. The concert by the band Queen and the two-day Polish Masters football tournament made a loss of 10 million zloties: tickets were given out for free to fill the stadium. The city of Poznań had to pay 3 million zloties extra for the opening concert by Sting. The concert by Jennifer Lopez in Gdańsk brought in a minimum profit, but none of the cities is willing to organize more events like those, because, as the operators declare, "you can't make money on them". In their opinion, a concert would be profitable if each ticket costs 400 zloties. Music agencies, on the other hand, are convinced that the problem is the lack of long-term plans and frequent changes in the boards of stadiums (Kokot and Karbowiak 2012). Moreover, the operators have experienced problems with renting VIP boxes and office spaces in the arenas (Kokot and Karbowiak 2012). The additional costs of the repairs, necessary due to the faults in the (often rapid and imprecise) construction process, have become a thorn in the City Council's side. In 2013, the city spent 2.2 million zloties on repairs to the stadium (Miasto może odzyskać pieniądze za remont 2014). In its budget for 2014, Poznań planned to spend an additional 3.7 million zloties on maintenance and further repairs (with total spending planned at 2.8 billion zloties with a planned surplus of 33 million) (Lipoński 2013c).

The operator of the city stadium has experienced difficulties paying its monthly rent to the city on a regular basis. Already in December 2012, "Gazeta Wyborcza" wrote about the club's debt and the operator of the stadium in one (Żytnicki 2012). The monthly rent which the club should have paid to the city amounted to 260,000 zloties. Lech Poznań had problems with paying it regularly ("Wyborcza" also intervened earlier to explain this situation). Moreover, it is the city (POSiR) which pays the club's bills for utilities (around 200,000 zloties per month); up to December 2012, POSiR paid 1.2 million zloties for water, electricity and gas at the venue.

The stadium has been managed by Lech Poznań and the Marcelin Management consortium since September 2011. Initially, it was supposed to be used by two local clubs, Lech and the second-league Warta

Poznań, but the clubs' boards were not able to reach an agreement and only the Kolejorz organizes its training and plays matches at the venue. Initially, the agreement signed between the city and the consortium for 20 years obliged the club to pay a monthly rent of 3.1 million zloties, 7.5% of profits from match days and 30% of the profits from sale of the rights to the name of the stadium (Stadion miejski w Poznaniu 2012). In May 2014, the agreement between the city and the operator of the stadium was renegotiated. Instead of paying an annual rent and agreed profits from match days, and bearing the costs of maintaining the venue, the operator agreed to pay only 600,000 zloties annually and 4% of the income from European and Champions League matches. Moreover, as a result of the negotiations, the city relinquished its 30% share in profits from the sale of the name of the venue – quite an unpleasant surprise, considering that the operator was simultaneously negotiating an agreement with a possible buyer. In June 2013, the club landed the first stadium naming rights deal, changing the name to the INEA Stadion until 2018 (INEA being a regional major telecommunication company). The local edition of "Gazeta Wyborcza" fiercely reacted to the way the stadium is maintained. Journalists were aware that "Lech cannot afford to pay a high rent, the city cannot afford to have an empty stadium . . . , [and] both sides are somehow fated to stay with each other" (Wesołek 2013; cf. Wesołek and Wybieralski 2012), but at the same time, they pointed to the discrepancy between the promises which the city made before Euro 2012 and what turned out to be a reality afterwards: "The city authorities, with mayor Grobelny at their head, have made us believe that the venue which is being built at Bułgarska will be multi-functional, perfect for organising concerts and events different to football matches. We were lured by the promise of the profits which can be made when hosting great stage stars. Yet this is all humbug (. . .). Why the citizens of Poznan were deliberately deceived is obvious – the goal was to justify the spending of much more than 700 million (. . .). Mayor Grobelny will have to figure out before the next elections how to explain to the citizens why the stadium which was built in such difficult times with their money is only going to be used by football fans, because it was supposed to be different" (Wesołek 2012; cf. Wesołek and Wybieralski 2012).

A representative of the city stadium's operator, whom I talked to some time after the championship, was not surprised by the public's reaction and accused the authorities of misleading people:

> I would put it this way . . . if you had a new car and had been told at the beginning that it had a projector which allows you to watch movies on the wall of your room, and sometime later you found out that, even though you had not been using this function, the projector had not been working, but you had paid extra money for it, how would you react? I am not surprised . . . everywhere in Poland the stadiums were promised to be multifunctional arenas where concerts could be organised . . . concerts which we needed so badly . . . but who promised that? Local authorities who had no idea about how a stadium is managed. I had no idea how it worked either before I came to Lech and saw how Marcelin Management managed the stadium, when it turned out that yes, there is a lot of office space at the stadium, but it is not suitable for most companies, because who would like to have dark offices, offices without windows? Or with windows, but with a view of a white membrane? There are companies who require spaces like those, but it is very difficult to find them. . . . So there are many things which had not been thought over, but this stadium still has great potential. Can you imagine that under the roof a tank battle can be organized? You can hang several original tanks there and organize a battle, it is the only stadium in Europe where you could do that, no other has this possibility. This is phenomenal! But again, you have to find someone who will take care of it, who will organize a battle.

The *business rationality* is here juxtaposed with the authorities' promises and people's expectations. The stadium can host not only international matches and serve as a concert venue, but it can also be the arena of a spectacular "tank battle". However, whether such events will take place depends on business calculation and entrepreneurial logic. Anyone who questions this has "no idea about how a stadium is managed", i.e. has no knowledge about making business.

Having said that, my interlocutor argues that no matter what the costs, the stadium is indispensable in a modern, European city.

Whatever people say, however disappointed they might be, this is a requirement which is absolutely essential in Poznań. When I asked why the city should pay for a stadium at all if it is too expensive to serve as a public venue, he gave me a forgiving look:

> Why? [pauses] And why does the city need a sewage system? Poznań still needs an arena for 20,000 people. Such places, stadiums, venues, all around the world are not built to make money. In Poland, when it was calculated how much the stadium would cost, some started to say that it should make money. No, this is a sort of investment... at least everywhere in the world... which has a promotional character... these costs have to be borne so other things could be happening. *Those people simply have to understand this is reality* [emphasis: mine].

From this perspective, the stadium should not be expected "to make money". Its role is first and foremost promotional and representative. It represents a certain vision of modernity, as we might have learned from then Prime Minister Donald Tusk's speech at the official opening of the National Stadium in Warsaw, who said: "I would like Poland in the future to be as modern as the National Stadium" (Kokot and Karbowiak 2012). Therefore, despite the financial problems, the event was declared a great success. The stadiums, the main venues of the Championship, were presented as symbols and an absolute necessity: a new "sewage system" of the modern city. This is *reality*, as my interlocutor stressed. The citizens simply *have to understand it*.

In general, after calculating the cost of the tournament (when it suddenly turned out that money had never been a goal for the organizers), the biggest achievement proved to be the promotional success and the suppression of the negative stereotype of Poles. "Gazeta Wyborcza" in Wrocław celebrated the fact that "our guests got to know a civilized country and its friendly inhabitants. An Irishman suddenly saw that a Polish immigrant living in his country has a beautiful homeland, where Irish kids could leave peacefully. Because we had the Czech team playing here, Wrocław had its individual contribution to changing Polish–Czech relations. In our neighbours' eyes, a Pole is a parochial Catholic and a lazy buffoon living in a poor and backward country without highways.

How surprised they were when during their stay in Wrocław a foreign man gave them champagne after the Czechs beat his national team, and hundreds applauded the Czech players in front of the Monopol hotel…. So screw the results, we won our Euro" (Sawka 2012). The same pride was shared by the media in Gdańsk, another host city, where "the four matches which we organized proved that we are not European provinces, that hosting the world's third biggest event is not a problem for us. What is more, we can do it better than the others" (Jamroż 2012).

After the championship, the local Tourist Office in Poznań discussed the effort which together with the town hall they had put into promoting the city in Croatia, Ireland and Italy – the countries whose national teams played in Poznań and from which the majority of visitors were expected. Promotion was not an easy task as Poland "was an undiscovered territory, a bit exotic for our guests…. Unfortunately, even now many people from the West think stereotypically that Poland is a post-communist and backward country. Euro shattered these misconceptions. All of sudden, it turned out that we are a normal European metropolis, that Poznań is just as cool as our guests' homes, or even more so" (Mazurczak 2012). The same representative of the Tourist Office recalled an interesting story which can serve as an example of the self-orientalizing practices which could have been observed during the event: "We were great hosts. Everyone wanted to have good fun here, not only the visitors, but also the locals. We presented ourselves as hospitable and helpful people. Citizens often approached foreign fans and asked whether they could have helped them. And the praise for volunteers was endless. I have also heard a story about a group of Poles who tried to offend some Irish and who were immediately pacified by those guys from Poznań, who did not want anyone to bring disgrace upon the city" (Mazurczak 2012). During Euro 2012, Poznań hosted 70,000 Irish guests, 40,000 Croatians and 15,000 Italians. According to the first estimates, the guests from Ireland spent 150 million euro in Poznań (Euro 2012, nr 1), and the Fan Zone was visited by 706,000 guests (Euro 2012, nr 1).

Rafał Drozdowski, a sociologist from Poznań, argued that "the citizens of Poznań and Poles in general needed proof that we are not as parochial as we think we are. Or as we reckon the others perceive us. We still think we are an inferior nation and that is where the provincial character of Poland comes from. Everything that happened on the Polish streets during Euro helps us to recover from this parochial inferiority complex. . . . For foreigners we are a normal country, neither a European pearl, nor the end of the group" (Drozdowski 2012). Mayor Grobelny argued that hosting sporting mega-events means *seizing a chance for a modernization jump*, even at the cost of running up a debt, as was the case when the General Exhibition was organized in Poznań (Grobelny 2012). Mayor Grobelny liked and eagerly compared Euro 2012 with the legendary exhibition from the interwar period. In this particular article, he also referred to governmental practices from the late 1970s, which, in his opinion, had mobilized cities to make spectacular investments: "Today we laugh at the proverbial painting of grass before harvest festivals under Gierek, but those events also stimulated the city to make improvements. . . . Now, Euro 2012 was this sort of motivation. . . . I am strongly convinced that mega-events are an idea which motivates us, gives us the strength and courage to make difficult decisions, and which let us bear the difficulties of construction work and overhauls". He probably did not realize that by referring to those practices of "powdering" the city from back in the times of communism, he gave his opponents yet another argument against himself. Already in 2007 critics of the event argued that the idea of hosting the event in Poland did not differ that much from the communist logic with its gigantomanic projects and monuments erected to the glory of the system (Achrem 2007; cf. Kowalska 2017). The protest committee Chleba Zamiast Igrzysk (*Bread Instead of Games*) compared the logic behind hosting Euro 2012 to Edward Gierek's politics in the 1970 (Chleba zamiast igrzysk 2012). Gierek, the First Secretary of the Polish United Workers' Party from 1970 to 1980 and as such the leader of the country, promised increasing availability of consumer goods and modernization of Poland. His reform was based on billion dollar loans from Western countries. This short-sighted and profligate politics led to the economic crisis at the end of 1970, the rise of the *Solidarity* movement and eventually to the collapse of the system. This comparison could not meet with sympathy in Poznań, traditionally proud of its economic rationality, entrepreneurial skills and "westernness".

The promotional aspects of the event (changing both the external and internal image of the country and its citizens) have been perceived as the main benefit of Euro 2012 (Deloitte 2012). One of the Ambassadors of Euro 2012 – a group of celebrities who promoted the event in the city and abroad – emphasized that tournaments like this are organized in countries which need them, such as South Africa or Brazil: "This is a chance to tell the world that Poland is a cool and modern country", he said, "and *no polar bears are running on its streets*". It is not only the stadium that the city "got": as elsewhere in the modern world, Euro 2012 was used as a "promotional vehicle" (Lowes 2002) to boost the city's image as a modern, European metropolis. This promotional strategy is deeply rooted in Poland's modernization discourse.

From Modernization Discourse to Civilizational Jump

In September 2007, the Polish edition of the Forbes magazine published an interview with Donald Tusk (Tusk 2007), at that time the leader of the opposition party Civic Platform (*Platforma Obywatelska*, PO). He criticized the government of the Prime Minister Jarosław Kaczyński, the leader of the Law and Justice party (*Prawo i Sprawiedliwość*, PIS). Although the interviewer insisted that Tusk had changed his views on the market economy and become less "liberal" than he used to be, he presented himself as a great admirer of the "free market, competition and private ownership", dreaming about building a "real democratic capitalism" in Poland. This was a time when Tusk talked openly about privatizing the social insurance institution (*Zakład Ubezpieczeń Społecznych*, ZUS) and the health care system. He also argued that "the government is to make sure that laws and rules are obeyed, not to interfere in the everyday course of the market game", and that "Poles who got to know the Irish, British or American reality have no doubts that the best friend for those who cannot cope with life is the free market, and that their worst enemy is state control". It will not be an exaggeration, therefore, contrary to the journalist's claims, to call his standpoint neo-liberal. When asked about Euro 2012, he made a remark which is particularly interesting when seen with the benefit of hindsight: "The government's optimism in seeing Euro 2012 as their big success and as a *key to rapid civilizational growth* is just one big load of nonsense. Poland and Ukraine got Euro 2012 without Polish government participation in the bidding process. There is no reason to kid ourselves, and the key role here was played by a certain wealthy Ukrainian. Euro 2012 is rather a huge obligation, which requires a lot of effort and resources. In a longer term, this investment effort will bring us benefits. But on one condition: those investments will not be monuments to the political greatness of city mayors nor to the Prime Minister. They really must be tailored to our abilities".

But that was back in September 2007. In October 2007, Civic Platform won its first Parliamentary election in Poland, and Donald Tusk became the new Prime Minister of the Republic of Poland. The "civilizational jump" became one of the key terms to explain all aspects of national politics. Almost six years after the interview quoted above, Donald Tusk declared that "his proposition is a safe, *steadily growing state* and a *gigantic developmental and civilizational jump*. Our goal is to bring the level or life and civilizational development closer to the West, to make Poland a real political, but also civilizational partner for the biggest and the wealthiest countries in the West". When asked about the ongoing conflict with the opposition party, PIS, he argued: "I am fundamentally convinced that Poland needs a strong centre. It turns people back from the ideological front lines, stabilizes the situation and concentrates on civilizational tasks. PO is tailored to those Poles who want an improvement in their fate and safety, not radical right- or left-wing battles. That is what we have always been" (Tusk 2013a: 15). He repeated his stance in an interview in July, where he said: "We [PO in opposition to PIS] refer to the rest, in its own diversity: to modern Poles in a modern world, who aspire to a civilizational jump...after the historical shift of the borders to the West we need to move these borders in people's emotions and minds. We need to abandon the legends and myths of the Eastern Borderlands and start to think more like people in Greater Poland, Pomerania, and Silesia. This should form the modern

Pole" (Tusk 2013b: 13). By saying this, Tusk flattered his electorate: the western (and former Prussian) regions of Poland voted for the liberal and pro-European Civic Platform (PO).

Catching up on "civilizational differences" also seemed to be an *idée fixe* of the advocates of the free market, as we can see in this interview with a Lead Economist for the Europe and Central Asia Region in the World Bank: "Let's not trust the false prophets who offer a shortcut to prosperity. We still think that the state should provide us with possibilities of work and with high salaries. But the state does not have such abilities. This is the role of entrepreneurs. Our salaries depend not on the state, but on catching up on the civilizational differences" (Rutkowski 2013). This rhetoric derives from orientalizing and self-orientalizing perspectives which see Poland as an underdeveloped, catching-up country, reclaiming its place in Europe in many areas: political, economic and cultural one. It prevailed in public discourses during different periods of history, as we saw in the previous chapter, but it became almost omnipresent when Poland entered the transition period from the communist system to the market economy, when it underpinned the neo-liberal turn (cf. Buchowski 2001, 2006; Stacul 2014; Kiel 2014).

An international sport mega-event was one of the greatest opportunities for Poland to "catch up" with the more developed West – and to prove that the country is indeed European, not eastern.

That is why Joanna Mucha, the Minister of Sport and Tourism of the Republic of Poland, although claiming elsewhere to be mostly concerned with everyday sport and not only its Olympic version (Mucha 2012), 6 months before the championship called Euro 2012 a "gargantuan civilizational jump forward" (Euro to boost economy 2012). And that is why the editor-in-chief of the weekly "Wprost", when discussing Polish inferiority complexes in his editorial before the Championship, asked his compatriots to be "good hosts": "Poland . . . is a country that is making its way, transforming fast in a good direction. *In a last-ditch attempt, in the Polish style*, we are finishing construction work which will endure for decades. Eventually, we may start to shed the inferiority complex of a poor relation. (. . .) We will not have another chance like this one in a long time" (Kobosko 2012). A former national team player claimed that "Euro 2012 is the most important sport event in the history of the country and we might not have another chance like this for a long time (Lubański 2012)". Euro 2012 became a sort of "state of emergency" (Woźniak 2013; cf. Hall 2006) and a political goal which required a broad consensus among political and business elites and the Polish media, including new legislatives.

However, there is a certain contradiction in this rhetoric. How can the vision of a *steadily* growing state which Donald Tusk was propounding in the interview justify the *civilizational jump*? And will this work which editor Kobosko praises in his editorial indeed "endure for decades", if it was built "in a last-ditch attempt, in the Polish style"? How could such a rhetoric resonate with the self-image of the citizens of Poznań? As in the rest of the country, the modernization discourses there were backed by the urge to distance Poland from the East and (re-)unite it with the West. But at the same time, Poznań considered itself to already be *more western* than the rest of country, and this *westernness* manifested itself in a certain style of doing things. As I will demonstrate, *jumping* or building *in a last-ditch attempt*, cobbled together at the last minute was not considered representative for this style.

Press analysis and interviews with decision-makers in Poznań show that the "civilizational jump" became indeed the leitmotif of the discourse of Euro 2012, a key term used to justify and legitimize the organization of the event. The motif of general mobilization was brought up in my conversation with a representative of the budget department at the City Hall, who pointed out that Euro 2012 was never meant to be the city's financial success, but rather served as a *kick* to modernize the country and the city. He also made a reference to the General National Exhibition, which confirms the status of the legendary fair as a landmark event in the city's history:

The main goal of Euro 2012 was to improve the infrastructure, it was a kick to mobilize us for a certain event, whose date could not be changed – and that has its pluses and minuses – but generally speaking, it was a moment of maximum mobilization. Mayor Grobelny in one of his speeches compared Euro 2012 to the PeWuKa from the inter-war period. It is difficult to compare these two events, as they were held in very different times, but they both caused this mobilization in the city; at that time, Poland developed a lot during the preparation period, then the war started, and now Euro 2012 was such an element, such an event which mobilized us to great investments, to catch up on decades, because it was not that all these things were done only for the Euro. Some of them had to be done anyway, maybe the stadium would not have been built had it not been for the Euro, or not on such a scale, we have quite a buoyant football club, which planned those investments but maybe not on a scale which enabled us to apply for hosting the event. Many other investments would have been completed anyway, but the Euro factor was the mobilizing one, a stimulating one, because thanks to certain activities addressed to the host cities and of hundreds of millions zloties of additional financing which we got, all that makes me see Euro 2012 as a civilizational kick. Thanks to the Euro, we managed to do certain things in the city; of course, it required taking out loans, but a lot of external resources were obtained. We can also speak of the promotional effect, we cannot underestimate it, I don't have any hard data here, but I read that tourist traffic probably increased after Euro. I think it was caused by the fact that Poznań appeared in the European consciousness as a place worth visiting, which is important because in fact it is not we who benefit from it, but it is the companies which operate here. It is not that the budget...if you asked me where the money is in the budget.... I must be straightforward, you will not see this money in the budget, the money is on the other side, under "spending", the profit is in small companies which dominate the market in Poznań, in the tourist and gastronomy sector, they turned up during the championship...It results in our economy growing.

This perspective clearly corresponds with the one which associates the well-being of Poles with narrowing the civilizational gap between Poland and the West. Euro 2012 is one of the moments which are seen as a "tremendous opportunity to catch up" (PWC 2011: 1) for Polish cities which "in many ways...still find themselves lagging behind the cities of western Europe that they seek to compete with and be compared to" (3). As my interlocutor said, the date of this "kick" could have not been changed and the momentum must have been used to "catch up on decades". But does a "jump" really have the same effect as (or can it be better than) years of steady, sustainable and well-planned development?

One of the most interesting conversations I had during my research was about the urban promotional strategy and policy. From the perspective of this civil servant, Euro 2012 was a milestone in the city's development process, and its legacy should be considered at least in three areas: promotional, civilizational and social.

> To my mind, Euro 2012 was a chance for Poznań to appear in Europeans' consciousness. To leave the level of a Polish city and become a European metropolis. The city develops only when it attracts new resources, such us capital, people and ideas. For a city to develop it must attract new ideas, and to attract new ideas it must compete with others in Europe, so it must gain a competitive position, and it can gain it only by becoming recognized as a brand in people's consciousness.
>
> This is vital, because in a way Euro 2012... confirmed that the city is able to organise even major undertakings. From my point of view, this is a crucial thing. The other aspect is the civilizational jump. The number of investments completed is... well, some compare it to the heyday of Poznań under mayor Cyryl Ratajski... and the standing which Poznań used to have back then. Of course, this investment would have been completed anyway, but surely in a much longer time frame. Thirdly, social engagement. The people who prepared the event, and I am not thinking only about the decision-makers, but also about the citizens, about volunteers... the citizens who took part in different initiatives in the course of preparing for the event. Because for us the Euro was a chance... it was an attempt to get into people's mentality, to *change this mentality*, to make them more open to the outside.... This equates to a civilizational jump.

The whole conversation indicated a strong correlation between "becoming a European metropolis", "civilizational" acceleration (understood as investment in a particular sort of infrastructure, such as roads, railway stations and airports) and "changing people's mentality". These three aspects are to decide on the future success of the city, until recently "an unknown, a no-name city", which is currently transforming into a Western "metropolis". This extract illustrates how the event was legitimized by reference to the local history of trade and the entrepreneurial tradition. My interlocutor compared "the Euro chance" to the interwar period, "the heyday of Poznań under mayor Ratajski" with its hallmark event: the legendary General National Exhibition. This reference aimed at showing the continuity between the interwar development (and

Golden Years of the city) and the "mobilization" before Euro 2012. The regional success – understood as boosting the city's attractiveness for attracting global capital and resources – was presented as a consequence of the city's pre-war development.

Moreover, the event was also a chance to "change people's mentality", to convince them to take part in such a regional success. Michael Hall notices that "the relative decline of importance of World Fairs and Expositions has gone hand-in-hand with the growth in the significance of sports mega-events for urban and regional growth and place competition" (2006: 60). Sport mega-events, similarly as big trade events before, are powerful tools of propaganda: they are intended to change the image, the form (infrastructure) and the people. Whitson and Horne (2006) argue that international mega-events, especially for provincial identities, can be understood as "occasions for self-representation, signaling the arrival of once marginal communities into membership in the dominant world order" (83). However, as the scholars continue, the primary target of promotional practices and discourses are not the visitors and international audience, but local citizens. Whitson and Horne propose that "the growth that local elites anxiously hope will result from the re-imagining of their cities does not follow from outside investment alone. What is also necessary is that a regional population who have traditionally been thought as provincial – *and have thought of themselves as provincial* – are encouraged to become more ambitious and outward-looking in their aspiration" (83; original emphasis). Those aspirations are primarily consumer ones. Mega-events are "not only about showing the city off to the world; it is also about putting the global on show for the locals, and inviting them to take on new identities as citizens of the world – identities that will henceforth be lived in the production and consumption of global products" (83).

Cities which were seen as provincial have a chance to reposition themselves as economically advanced on different scales, nationally and internationally (Whitson and Horne 2006: 81). In Canadian examples described by Whitson and Horne (quoting various scholarships), the Olympic host societies were "invited to 'think big', to look beyond their traditional regional horizons, to make themselves into national, even global leaders [Calgary] ...; to shine on a global stage [Alberta]; ... [or] to identify with the 'spirit of achievement' [Vancouver]" (82). Whitson and Horne stress that "investment in civic image is believed to be crucially important in attracting capital and people 'of the right sort'" (81; cf. Harvey 1989) because "the attraction of outside money is believed to depend increasingly upon civic image. . . . Important signals are sent to outside investors about wealth and organizational competence, and about governments that work effectively with the private sector" (83). This dimension of the promotional effect of the tournament was raised in the press extracts about Euro 2012 which I quoted above. This was also, as explicitly expressed by the same interlocutor of mine, the goal of the organizers of Euro 2012:

> We wanted to convince people that everyone can be a host, and that it is up to them how the city will be perceived, not only the matches, but also the investments, the atmosphere. It was a "joint venture", between the city and the citizens, and we wanted people to think about it that way. So we tried to make people think positively, and success was possible because they joined us, because our cause was supported by many, by the young and the old. It proved that there is great potential within society, that we are able to organise big events, that we are an open community. . . . And in fact, our aim was to change people's attitudes, make them think less about "I, now" and more about "we". . . . Euro was a tool of communication. We wanted to reach people and try to change their mentality. It did not mean we wanted to tell them what to think, rather we tried to convince them that we are one community and should achieve certain goals together. . . . I cannot tell now whether it worked well, it is too early, but I would risk saying that it is slowly starting to work, that something is changing in people's mentality.

The goal of the event was to change people's mentality, to convince them to share the same ideas – in order "to achieve certain goals together". Hence the motto of the Euro promotional campaign: *Wszyscy jesteśmy drużyną narodową*, We all are the national team. This was part of the campaign which, in words of Kimberley Schimmel, was "designed to legitimate the actions of urban growth coalitions by expressing them as being necessary for the betterment of the community-as-a-whole . . . a campaign that not only seeks to promote the interests of the dominant class but also seeks to legitimize political solutions to urban 'problems' by symbolically constructing consensus...behind the banner of pro-growth" (Kimberly Schimmel 1995, after Lowes 2002: 82–3).

Bea Vidacs argues, "extending [Benedict] Anderson's thesis on the rise of nationalism, [that] football is a major force in imagining the nation" (Vidacs 2010: 87). Euro 2012 was also seen as a chance to "change people's mentality", to encourage them to support the great national cause: building the image of a modern, European state. In Poznań, the "civilizational jump" was seen as a chance to fill in the gap between the golden years of the interwar period and the rebirth of the entrepreneurial spirit in 1989. The decision-makers saw themselves as heirs to the legendary interbellum, hence the comparisons made between Euro 2012 and the General Exhibition, and between mayor Grobelny and the legendary Cyryl Ratajski. The tournament was therefore the result of a consequent strategy which promoted Poznań as a business-friendly location. Although it was about to reveal to what extent this strategy is embedded in the Poznań's *genius loci*, it was introduced as an undisputed sign of city's modernity and both political and economic rationality.

There Is No Alternative

When I talked about the goals and results of the event with a representative of Euro Poznań 2012, a municipal company responsible for preparing the Championship in the city, one of her first statements was: "We put a lot of effort into showing that this is not a polar bear country". In her opinion, similar to that of others engaged in organizing the tournament, the event was a great chance to modernize the city and promote it as a European location. For them, the decision to host Euro 2012 was pretty self-explanatory and *commonsensical*, as contemporary cities have little alternative if they want to take part in the global competition. That point of view resembles that of Ryszard Grobelny, the mayor of Poznań, who, when asked about the city spending and budgetary cuts after Euro 2012, could not "imagine that a *rational* citizen would think that all this [infrastructure] was unnecessary" (Ponad 20 mln debetu 2012). Norman Fairclough sees these statements as examples of the results of the naturalization process of a certain type of discourse, which then becomes something natural, something so obvious that no discussion is needed. He calls naturalization "the royal road to common sense. Ideologies come to be ideological common sense to the extent that the discourse types which embody them become naturalized. . . . What comes to be common sense is . . . to a great extent determined by who exercises power and domination in a society or a social institution. But in the naturalization of discourse types and the creation of common sense, discourse types actually appear to *lose* their ideological character" (Fairclough 2001: 76; original emphasis). When I asked my interlocutors to comment on the arguments against the event, they often sighed, shrugged their shoulders or got irritated. The pro-Euro standpoint, on the contrary, was simply right, rational and proved to be successful, as the following extract from my conversation with the representative of the organizing company clearly shows. One of the anti-Euro arguments was that is sucked the money from the public purse and resulted in budgetary cuts in the public sector, including education. I asked my interviewee whether she could comment on any correlation between spending on the Euro and cuts in other areas of the budget. She replied:

[Answer]   We will not regret [that we decided to take the challenge] because a city which does not engage in organizing such big events simply does not develop. The discussions on the budget for such events and for education are two unrelated issues. Of course, if people who earn 1,000 or 1,500 zloties in kindergartens were here now, they would probably get angry, but big cities are indebted, all of them; in most of them there are some budget shortfalls, and the one in Poznań is not the result of Euro 2012. . . . The reason why there are budget gaps in education *is not because we had Euro 2012, but because the budget is too small.* I would probably be attacked by educational circles, but we have to separate these two things. Why is London organising the Olympics? London is such a renowned city, well-prospering and beautiful, why is it doing this? This is all in order to maintain the image of an energetic, open city, with certain principles, promoting sport, having a certain vision. I cannot imagine any developing city would avoid organising big events that strengthen its image and attract people from all over the world. . . . We cannot regret that we organised an event which was noticed all over the world . . . , because it brings long-term promotional and financial benefits; because the city sent a message to the world that it should be considered a metropolis, a developed city, full of young and beautiful people. And we played the game and will not lose it. I mean, we may lose it if we stop being seen like that. Of course, it is not a 1:1 financial success, but we have to remember that money invested in railway stations, roads, the stadium, the airport.... I don't think there is anyone who would rather find himself at the old railway station and would be happy if there were fewer flight connections with Europe. One of the commercial TV stations in Poznań kept on repeating that these investments were for Euro 2012 – no, these are investments for the city. They will remain in the city, the Euro was a catalyst, it helped us to get decisions and means, we could have lived with the old station and airport, we still could have old streets and it could have been dirty, but that is not the point. Let's show ourselves from the best side, this is our aim, it will stay with us for long. Poznań built an image of a European metropolis, a developed city. This is the benefit.

[Question]   And you do not have any doubts whether organising such an event was rational in a city of the size of Hannover? London could afford the Olympics, but Poznań?

[A]   I will put things differently – when Chorzów and Cracow [two reserve cities] took part in the beauty contest and we were worried that Cracow would win the event . . . what would have happened if Poznań had given up and Cracow had won the Euro? How many questions, how many accusations that we did not make it, how much could we have achieved.... I think we would have been eaten alive by the press. I am saying it as a city representative. The councillors would have had a very different attitude than today and shouted that we had had lost our chance. This tendency has changed, everything depends on the point of view. Everything stays with us, the investments were our goal and I do not think there would be many people eager to pass this success to Cracow.

[Q]   So . . . you are saying that there is no alternative?

[A]   This is well said. . . . We either go for it, or we hide at the back. We need a kick to start the infrastructural change in the city, and we need a kick to draw other countries' attention. In my opinion, there is no alternative. Of course, it must stand up and be linked to other needs in the city, but I don't see any possibility to give up organising big events, I think it would be unfavourable, even harmful to the city . . . , now everybody will pick at the "Barcelona effect", not understanding what it really means, and it is about how the perception of a city can be changed and what was done to the city, we even call it a "Poznań effect", precisely because this is a chance for the city to invest in development and appear on the global arena. *I can't imagine giving up such events.*

As we can see, a modern city which wants to be competitive must seize the chance and organize an event like Euro, no matter the budget limitations. There is no alternative if it wants to develop. Should we adopt the entrepreneurial perspective, it is difficult to argue with the argument that the city needs to invest in key infrastructural projects (the stadium, the railway station, the airport, new roads and tramlines) and in promotional campaign, which attract globally mobile capital and investors. This all builds the city's brand, both worldwide and within the country, at least at the promotional level (cf. Jessop 2013 [1997]; 2013 [1998]). Moreover, it is hard to gainsay the fact that some parts of the city benefited and grew before Euro 2012. Even the urban cyclists, usually in opposition to Grobelny's politics (favouring car transportation rather than public or bikers), must have admitted that they enjoyed riding new lanes built on Bukowska street. But, as I will show in the next chapter, this has been criticized too, as part of a certain vision of the city, which, according to the opposition, in the long term does not serve the interests of the majority of citizens.

This "no-alternative" perspective on Euro 2012, understood as a chance to present the region in the world arena, was also explicitly expressed by one of the Ambassadors of the Championship whom I talked to about the legacy of the event. Interestingly, in our conversation, he referred to certain "characteristics of the Polish culture": the ability to mobilize in a short time to achieve great goals. This statement may bring connotations of the long history of the (usually unsuccessful) Polish insurrections and uprisings, which, as a careful reader might remember, in Poznań are juxtaposed with the tradition of organic work. But my interviewee thought about more recent examples of "uniting beyond political differences", such as the Great Orchestra of Christmas Charity (*Wielka Orkiestra Świątecznej*

Pomocy, WOŚP, the biggest non-governmental, non-profit charity organization in Poland), which served as a more positive point of reference in the discourse of the civilizational jump:

> Poznań could have never afforded to spend such an amount of money on promotion had it not hosted Euro 2012. Right, we still have tumbledown buildings in Łazarz and Wilda [city districts], but the money which was spent on the Euro would have never been spent on those neighbourhoods. Besides, places like those can be found in every city, in Berlin, and in Paris, too. We are a nation that always complains, yet, after all, when we have a goal, we know how to motivate ourselves, we managed to build the infrastructure, which we could not have built for several years, for decades. We were united, as during WOŚP, beyond political differences. I do not understand why people do not notice the fact that we managed to accomplish so much in such a short time. And we would not have had money for kindergartens anyway.

There was, as we can read in these two quotes, no possibility that the money spent on promotion and organization of the event could have been spent on anything else, not within the political framework of the city which privileges promotion over welfare distribution, as put bluntly by the interviewee:

> We can build kindergartens and nurseries [and] playgrounds, but in my opinion they will not attract new resources to the city and they will not keep people in the city, now when they are moving to the suburbs.... I am not saying this is not important, but I am not sure if kindergartens are more important than promoting the city and attracting new resources. It is always a question of what results this will bring.

My interlocutors from the town hall were always taken aback when I tried to talk with them about the opposition's arguments. One of the civil servants became extremely angry when I confronted him with the argument that Euro 2012 fostered the growing city's indebtedness:

> Let's agree that I will not comment on these accusations. I really do not understand them. They are below my standard ... and I do not mean that I have higher standards, I am just saying I do not get such arguments.

That we have nothing left but loans to pay.... What kind of argument is it? *It is not supported by any facts...any knowledge.* Everyone has a right to think what they want, but I do not feel that I am obliged to try to convince them that my point of view is the right one...but I think it is a typical example of discontent, and grumbling.... There are two sorts of people, people who always see the glass half-empty and those who see it half-full.... I always try to look for positives and I get angry when I listen to people who are complaining about everything...when I read posts on the internet...people get annoyed, *they make remarks on things they know nothing about...they have no idea, they have no knowledge....* I do not want to forbid them speaking their minds, but they should get some knowledge before they make all those judgements.... I cannot stand listening to people who make all those *negative comments which are not justified by any knowledge*...it simply makes me angry.

This extract provides evidence of how the opposition was discredited as lacking knowledge and "having no idea". "They should get some knowledge before they make all those judgments" is a complementary statement to that of the stadium's representative quoted above, who argued that "people simply should understand that this is the reality". This resembles Fairclough's discussion on the discrediting practices in the struggles between the dominant and the dominated discourses: the intellectuals having a particular role in securing the hegemony, disregard opponents' arguments as making no sense, incomprehensible, being based on little knowledge on the "real situation".

Some of my interlocutors openly admitted that they were firm believers in the free market, as the civil servant quoted above: "I am a liberal", he said, "I do not want anything from the government.... I believe in myself and I do not want anything from anyone...everyone should take care of oneself and make no harm to others". From their point of view, the city should organize big events and invest in infrastructure, because this is the only way for it to attract outside resources – the main goal of the local politics. The less the state's or local government's interventionism, the more private and individual initiatives there are, and the better for the city development. When I asked one of the city's civil servants why the city keeps on selling plots to investors who want to build new shopping malls, he replied that the city did not decide on what is built and where: the market does. Had there been no demand for the malls, they would have not been built. "Have any of them been closed?", he asked rhetorically, and when I denied, he concluded with satisfaction: "There you go".

When I asked in the City Hall what they thought about those who criticized the city for hasty and therefore overpriced investments, another civil servant reacted in a fierce way. He was also indignant at the argument that in the case of Euro 2012, we could talk about privatizing profits and socializing costs, for instance, by cutting back on the welfare and education budget:

> It must have been said by someone who cannot count at all. First, most of the investment was financed by EU money anyway. It is not that I can build something whenever I want or wait to start it whenever I want. . . . Neither Euro 2012, nor the European budget would have waited. . . . Second, nowhere in the world are public finances on such a level that they could be spent on anything you want. So the critics say that we would have had more money of education if we had not been hosting Euro 2012? It is another original economic absurdity. We earned money on Euro 2012, in all respects: promotional, social, businesses made money, and we had an increase in investment. We did not make Euro for education. . . . If someone says we could have more money for education, I recommend him to open his own business and see how it works. If you want to make money, first you have to invest. If I want to work as a photographer, I have to buy myself a camera, otherwise I will not make money out of it. It is exactly the same with the city budget. Today, Poland develops so well comparing to Europe because we had this impulse, we had Euro 2012. . . . In general, if a city wants to develop, it must invest. If we stop investing, of course we have more money in the wallet, but we stop developing. This is the core . . . of basic economic knowledge. . . . So what you say is not a rational economic criticism.

The opponents pointed that the money spent on the stadium and promotion should have been spent on other aspects of the social life, such as public transportation, (social) housing and education, not to mention several infrastructural projects not listed as priorities before the tournament and not undergoing the refurbishment. They were discredited by the authorities either as lacking knowledge about how a modern city works, or as adherents of the old and long-gone system (socialists who always lay claims to something) or as guided by emotions. The stadium itself was often criticized as too big, too expensive or simply unnecessary. For many critics, it was a symbol of the elitist, privatized *governmentality* in the city: the power-holders should have called upon democratic tools (such as referendum or public consultations) when deciding how the money should be spent. The football club's representative could not agree on that:

> OK, but I am gonna tell you how it is. Very often...maybe it will sound critical, but anyway...if I had shared my information on the club with the journalists, there would have been millions of critical comments right away. Because it is not easy, we say it straightforwardly, the City has no money either and we need to economize on everything. People start to understand it, and let's say the best thing to do would be to say it out loud. But then...there is this question *whether the public can actually understand everything...public opinion is guided by emotions.* Football fans, for instance, are guided by emotions. We may use rational arguments, but sometimes it is better to speak about emotions...it reaches them faster and has a better impact...of course, underneath there must be some rational premises, but...you know. Similar rules apply to politics.... At the end of the day, people go to vote and are guided by their emotions, they look at who is nice, who is unfriendly, and vote for this and that...it is a beauty contest-...it is not about whether someone will be a good host...*the question is, whether people are experts in politics and governance, and whether they can rationally justify someone's work...the work of people who are in charge of the city today. It is, let's be honest, a rhetorical question, of course, the answer is "no, they are not", because where would they have this knowledge from...*And this is how it looks.

The city elites, including business and managerial class involved in organizing the event, were not interested in public discussion with the citizens. This standpoint clearly makes a distinction between those who know and should decide, and those who have no knowledge, are guided by emotions (not rational calculation) and should not get involved in the process of governing. When pointed out that then these decisions do not necessarily serve the general public, but only the interests of certain groups who owned the power, my interlocutor replied that the Euro was a chance to everyone who could seize the chance:

> Well, you cannot make everyone happy. It is like in this old joke, if you do not play lottery, you cannot win. We played and won. And of course there are people who are always very negative, people who prefer to take little steps, but when you see a challenge, you have to go for it. I think that *Euro 2012 was a great chance for everyone with a business idea.*

Those paragraphs demonstrate the elites' perspective, which is a result of crossing certain views and beliefs: that of individual freedom and entrepreneurialism, of the superiority of the market, of the need to attract outside resources to the city to increase its competitiveness and all that supported by the image *of the business character of the city and its citizens.* Criticism understood as personal or emotional is here opposed to economic rationality. Anyone with "basic economic knowledge" must agree with and support the city's *expertise* and *rational* strategy, which should be continued for the sake of urban development.

From this point of view, citizens and their activity are understood as the guarantors of the continuance of the economy-led and growth-oriented system. Hence, the idea of "changing their mentality", convincing them to support the cause, making them believe that "We all are the national team". They got a chance to "get rid of their socialist mentality" and become proactive, modern Europeans. This goal was justified by a reference to the articulated tradition of local entrepreneurialism – and this is how we should understand claims that the tournament was beneficial to everyone with a business idea, i.e. a typical, enterprising citizen of Poznań. As such, Euro 2012 was a grand *governmentality* project (Foucault 1997; Rose 1999; Rose et al. 2006; Shore and Wright 2011). The civic activity of citizens is desirable only in a narrow field: to help the power-holders to maintain the political status quo.

Furthermore, the inhabitants of the city are not desired as citizens, but more as consumers. As scholars note, mega-events change cities into consumer sites. They are, as argued on the previous pages, major tools in shifting the local politics from distribution and social obligation towards promotion and increasing the city's consumer and investment potential. As Swyngedouw et al. state, "cities are, of course, brooding places of imagination, creativity, innovation, and the ever new and different. However, cities also hide in their underbelly perverse and pervasive processes of social exclusion and marginalization and are rife with all manner of struggle, conflict, and often outright despair in the midst of the greatest affluence, abundance, and pleasure" (Swyngedouw et al. 2002: 545). Of course, not all citizens of Poznań could afford participation in sport spectacle, and not all of them can afford access to the "City of Play". Those who cannot are not as valued as those who can. Euro 2012 was one of those tools which accentuated and influenced further polarization in the city: between those who have power and those who do not; those who have a political voice and those who do not; and those who can make use of the new leisure facilities and those who cannot afford them. But at the same time, it also sharpened the polarization between two visions of the city.

The dominant narrative sold by the elites has not been bought by everyone in the city. The most radical critique of the event was probably made by the Anarchistic Federation and related anti-systemic or left-wing associations, which joined forces and organized a protest against the tournament (Buchowski and Kowalska 2015). But many other voices and concerns were raised before, during and especially after the end of the championship (cf. Mergler and Pobłocki 2010). Moreover, within the City Council, the mayor's policy was subjected to gradually fiercer and stronger criticism. During the budgetary session in December 2013, the Council discussed public investment in two major sports venues in Poznań: the city stadium and Termy Maltańskie (the Olympic swimming pool complex with thermal spa and saunas built before the Euro). The budget project envisaged paying extra 3 million zloties for maintenance of the pools and 3.7 million zloties for the overhaul of the stadium (Minutes 61 2013). One of the city councillors compared the mayor to an Egyptian pharaoh who built sport venues instead of pyramids. Mayor Grobelny had been compared to pharaoh previously (Grobelny buduje piramidy 2012; Minutes 36), but this time he replied that he had never hidden his plans of rebuilding the stadium, and that the citizens supported them by voting for him in the last election. Besides, he added, the stadium would not last as long as the pyramids of Giza. To that, another councillor sneered in reply: "Well, Mr. Mayor, what can we say: like pharaoh, like pyramid" (Minutes 61 2013; Lipoński 2013b).

4

"The City Is Not a Company". Or Is It?

Sports mega-events are never only about sport. They have always been, as other mega-events and megaprojects, also powerful propaganda tools. In Poland, including my field site in Poznań, Euro 2012 was used to legitimize spending public money (city resources and the EU funds) on the type of infrastructure crucial for attracting globally mobile capital and investment to the city, and for the promotion of the city as a business-friendly environment (which, in turn, aims to attract capital). This was done without broad public discussion on the pros and cons of hosting the event or public consultation on social needs and priorities. Euro 2012 was a "promotional vehicle" of a particular ideology and a tool used to sustain the *status quo* of power relations. It was also instrumental in strengthening the centralized, project-oriented and elitist type of governance and management.

Contrary to what some city councillors remaining in opposition to the mayor Grobelny told me, I argue that the Championship was not a spontaneous or *ad hoc* initiative. It was rooted in a long-term, entrepreneurial perspective on urban management and development, which has been shared by political and business elites over the last

© The Author(s) 2017
M.Z. Kowalska, *Urban Politics of a Sporting Mega Event*,
Football Research in an Enlarged Europe,
DOI 10.1007/978-3-319-52105-3_4

decades since the Polish transition from a centrally planned to a market system. As I tried to show in the previous chapters, the perspective could develop as it was linked with and embedded in the entrenched beliefs and stories about the entrepreneurial character of the city. This embeddedness justified why the city, "renowned for its tradition of good economy, high work discipline and frugality effectively uses the favourable circumstances after the systemic and economic transformation in Poland (. . .) and remains one of the leading economic centres in the country" (Raport o stanie miasta 2013: 5). But, as already indicated before, Euro 2012 was challenged as an event, whose organization and legacy did not fit the traditional image of the city. As such, it opened a sort of "communicative field" (Holmes 2014), where the practice was negotiated with the local beliefs, sentiments and expectations.

The Critique

One of the main objections raised by the opposition in Poznań was economic. The pro-Euro forces promoted the tournament as beneficial to the whole community, but the critics of this rhetoric argued that the championship was dedicated to affluent customers, not to the general public. Sports mega-events, as I argued in the previous chapters, are projects which serve the people who run them: "The most direct beneficiaries [of hosting mega-events]", write Whitson and Horne about the Olympic Games, are "construction companies and suppliers, engineers and architects, local security firms, media outlets, and anyone professionally involved in the promotional economy that now surrounds any Olympics (advertising, marketing, public relations)" (Whitson and Horne 2006: 84). The possible benefits usually bypass taxpayers (75). For instance, the sporting venues, despite previous pledges, do not serve the whole community as public facilities. In Poznań the stadium is used only by one professional team, and only at the beginning did it serve as a venue for one-off commercial events, which proved to be too expensive to be organized in the future.

Whitson and Horne link the production of an infrastructure for urban leisure (including sport venues) with the rise of entrepreneurial style of urban politics: "This has seen urban and regional governments compete with one another to offer incentives to private developers. . . . As a result, developers of professional sports venues and other upscale entertainment facilities have been able to extract public subsidies and tax holidays from governments anxious for their business, even while the same governments have been cutting back spending on social services. Neo-liberal political ideologies have brought market-oriented meanings to agendas like 'community development', as well as new definitions of the public good. There has been a shift away from notions of citizenship that stressed 'social rights', towards discourses of consumerism in which citizens are positioned as individual consumers of services, and the best cities are those that have 'world-class' shopping" (Whitson and Horne 2006: 76). Before the Euro, the elites united under the banner of one national cause – "We all are the national team" – and all citizens were encouraged to support the project of building the image of an open, prosperous metropolis, but the government concentrated not on broad social goals, but on revamping certain parts of the city addressed and accessible to affluent visitors and customers. The most radical critics argued that as a result, the city was divided between those who could make use of the new infrastructure and leisure centres on a daily basis, and those who could not afford them. Under such circumstances, purchasing power becomes people's main value as citizens (cf. Lowes 2002, Schimmel 1995). The "opportunity costs", as Whitson and Horne call them (2006: 77), were borne by poorer citizens who depended on efficiently functioning public services: these were reduced in order to pay for infrastructure, consulting and other event-related services. The local budget for public roads and transportation, as well as that for schooling, were decreased after the Euro. The education budget for the year following Euro 2012 was decreased by 20 million zloties – roughly the equivalent of the direct cost of the tournament (Brakuje 51 milionów 2012; Cięcia w budżecie 2012; Euro 2012, nr 2).

Whitson and Horne also warn against overestimating the benefits of the events, which the power-holders present as obvious and self-explanatory. They argue that such benefits should be analysed in the long term and in relation to the broad economic and political context (Whitson and Horne 2006: 77–80). For instance, the tourist boom is difficult to sustain in the years following an event; and the civic economy does not benefit from hosting the events to the extent it could if they were regular, annual events of an established reputation; the jobs created are usually temporary and of low quality (79). The authors also observe that the advertising benefits from the event are very dubious; moreover, they are preceded by spending realized in the years leading up to event, paid from public money (80). Some of my interlocutors pointed that the fans usually remember the country in which the event took place, but they forget the names of cities, and nobody knows where exactly in South Africa or in Austria the previous championships took place. The input, therefore, does not translate into any permanent benefit, not only in the case of the expensive stadium, but also that of promotion. Moreover, as I showed in the previous chapter, the initially estimated cost of the event and investments turned out to be highly deceptive. As Flyvbjerg et al. notice (2003), "over-optimistic forecasts of viability are the rule for major investments, rather than the exception" (43). Euro 2012 was advertised as a project which will generate economic growth in general, but, as various scholarships prove, mega-events usually benefit only certain groups of citizens, whereas the costs are borne by the taxpayer in general, also because "the misrepresentation of costs is likely to lead to misallocation of scarce resources, which, in turn, will produce losers among those financing and using infrastructure" (20). This is how the outcome of the event is presented by its opponents.

The profit and loss account of Euro 2012 was criticized as unfavourable to the community as a whole, and favourable only to the very small group of beneficiaries. The economic critique of the event is particularly interesting, because it unveils one of the biggest paradoxes of the Euro discourse in Poznań: the official political and media narrative, usually very concerned with economic figures, turned a blind eye to the often inefficient way in which many infrastructural investments were completed before Euro 2012. Not only the stadium but also investments such as the railway station or new tramlines have been criticized as being built sloppily and in haste, and therefore more costly than they would have been had they been carefully planned. This lack of consistency appears especially striking in Poznań, which prides itself on being an economic, a "German-like" city.

This disparity was revealed in my conversation with a civil servant and a football fan in one. We had earlier discussed the premises of "Against Modern Football",[1] and my interlocutor revealed that he had not been interested in the sport aspect of the championship, because Euro 2012 "is nothing more than a commercial event: it has a customer, not a fan, and we at the AMF are strongly against this". Then he moved on to discuss the positive effects of hosting the event. He differentiated between the perception of Euro as a football event and as a modernization boost, the latter being a great chance for the city. He enumerated investments completed or currently being completed in Poznań and argued that it was probably easier and cheaper to build them on account of the Euro (cf. Woźniak 2013). But as we spoke, he started to criticize the way the event was organized, and certain investments realized, including the city stadium, whose size was also criticized by football fans before the championship.

> We, the fans, *Wiara Lecha* [Lech Poznań' official fan club], draw attention to the fact that Poznań requires a stadium for 35,000 people maximum. But the authorities would always answer that they are building a stadium not for 10, but for 15, 20 years, when the needs will be bigger. But this is a mistake. It is better to have a smaller stadium, but one that is always full rather than a bigger one which is only filled every now and then.... What's more, UEFA did not require us to build a premium stadium like the one holding 44,000 in Poznań. There was no need for that, because we knew we would not host the quarter-final, the semi-final, nor the final.... It was because the out-of-control ambitions of the people who were deciding what stadiums must be built. This is my personal view. These people are my superiors, but this is my thesis. Someone simply lost themselves in this gigantomania. This was completely unnecessary.

---

[1] Against Modern Football has not been mentioned before in the book, although it often came up in my conversations. AMF's motto "Hate the business – love the game" aptly explains the movement's philosophy, i.e. standing against the ongoing commercialization and privatization of football.

In the same manner, he then derided the infamous tramline, the "tramline to IKEA" – as it is called by its critics – completed as a Euro investment, which did not reach the isolated parts of the city and whose last stop before the terminus is a shopping mall; and the new railway station, which he called, referring to the architecture of the building, "yet another ciabatta: Poznań is the city of ciabattas, we have the stadium and this ugly station, it all could have been done better". It turns out that according to him, only few investments could be perceived as relevant, well planned and properly managed, with the others being inadequate or of poor standard.

An example of even fiercer critique derives from my conversation with an influential businesswoman. We sat in her spacious office and talked about urban politics in general, as she had her own problems with dealing with the City Hall in the past. She regretted that the city officials had not learned from businesspeople and claimed that they had known nothing about long-term investment strategy and sustainable city politics. When asked whether hosting mega-events like the Euro is a good idea, she answered:

> It probably can be, on condition that it is based on economic calculations, where we could justify whether the expenditures, for instance, on the stadium, will pay off in the returns on those investments, if they are for the benefit of all citizens, anything. In my opinion, monstrous expenditure on the stadium will never be repaid. It is an exceptionally bad architectural design, which will bring no benefits but only additional costs to the city, because once something is built, it has to cost money.... I cannot see any benefits of Euro 2012, people who counted on some profits, hoteliers, restaurateurs, they all were disappointed, so I think it is not only my opinion, but of the citizens in general. Moreover, these particular actions should be followed by consistent actions in the future.... I don't know, maybe the city sees certain benefits of this event. I don't, except those negative consequences such as the stadium, maybe it resulted in some long-term contacts, in tourists who will leave some money in the city purse, maybe I don't know it, but it does not seem to me that it affected the city in any significant way.

Both those standpoints refer to the event as poorly planned and economically unprofitable. My interviewees refuse to see Euro 2012 as an evident success as it was not based on careful planning which would serve the city. And as Jessop argues, the promotional aspect of the event, i.e. creating the brand of an entrepreneurial metropolis is not convincing enough if not grounded in economic rationality and long-term planning on the part of the city officials (cf. Jessop 2013 [1997]; 2013 [1998]). This, I argue, had a tremendous impact on the evaluation of the event and the overall strategy of the urban politics.

In 2007, city councillors, many of them members of parties in opposition to mayor Grobelny, were happy that Poland, together with Ukraine, had won the Euro bid. They saw the tournament as confirmation that Poznań had become "accepted" as a European city. As one councillor told me, Poland is a "catching-up" country, which constantly climbs from the dark past of its often tragic history up to the "brave new world" of European standards and prestige. He saw the event as a proof that the country is on the right track and hoped that it would promote Poznań as a mature city which is able to organize big events like this one. Notwithstanding this initial applause, from the two elements of the "civilizational jump", the leitmotif of the championship rhetoric, most of the city councillors I interviewed bought only the civilizational part. Their perspective is similar to that of the two interlocutors of mine whom I quoted before: the civil servant football fan and the businesswoman. They all described Poland as a "catching-up country", and Euro 2012 as a chance to speed up modernization processes. They were concerned with infrastructural development and saw it as a desirable process on Poznań's way to becoming a European metropolis. They noticed and acknowledged some positive aspects of hosting the event: revamping certain parts of the city, developing the airport, speeding up many investments. At the same time, they remained suspicious of the narrative which presented Euro 2012 as a *kick* indispensable for the city to grow and thrive.

The same councillor who saw the Euro as proof that Poland is on the right track of development later voted against hosting yet another sporting event in the city, presented by the mayor as another promotional chance for Poznań. In the autumn of 2012, a few months after Euro 2012, when the Mayor of Poznań asked the City to support him in the bid to organize the 2018 Youth Olympic Games (YOG), and in borrowing 77 million zloties for this purpose, he was supported by only four councillors. Twenty seven voted against the YOG. The voting was preceded by a heated discussion on the city's debt and the rationale behind organizing another sporting mega-event (MIO 2018 nie 2012; Grobelny chce milionów 2012; cf. Kowalska 2016). It was criticized by the Council as an *ad hoc* proposition, expensive in terms of preparation and a burden on the city budget. It also prompted discussion about the need for long-term planning in urban management: megaprojects should not be seen as a goal in themselves, but they should be part of a deliberate strategy. This was not the case with Euro 2012, as my interlocutor claimed:

> The question is, how we will use the success [of Euro 2012]? We only had three matches in Poznań. The thing is, I am not saying we should not organise new mega-events . . . but it requires reorganising the whole municipal administration. Especially now, when many cities are out of breath because of the crisis, we should first and foremost think of a plan. I recently had a little argument with the Mayor, *when he compared Youth Olympic Games to the General National Exhibition. It is a clear misuse. Euro 2012 was also compared to this legendary exhibition*, sports mega-events are seen as equally important as this legendary fair. We should not jump from one event to another: all events should complement our development strategy. The city should have a sound urban strategy, it should improve the quality of life, because this is the key to everything, it makes people want to live in the city, binds them to the city and will eventually attract new investments. Therefore for me what's most important is the vision, and we should then choose the events which suit this vision. The city is not only the mayor, the Town Hall, it is all of us. All activities should be open to as many subjects as possible. Then the events are part of a bigger project, they support it. . . . Every event tells us something about the character of the city.

This perspective refers to attracting resources as a key tool in the modernization process, but it appreciates investment only as long as it is part of a plan and a vision. Short-term coalitions of politicians and business representatives should not replace a long-term "development strategy". This extract shows that what was questioned by some was not only the project-oriented mode of governance but also the comparison which the mayor made between Euro 2012 (or other sport events) and the General Exhibition from 1929. By referring to the success of the Exhibition, the authorities tried to legitimize the organization of the event and present themselves as heirs to the prosperous interwar period. Their opponents undermined this relationship as a *misuse*. General Exhibition – as a trade event, held on already existing premises and stimulating new investments in the interwar Poznań – was rooted in the entrepreneurial tradition of the city. Moreover, it opened a new chapter of its entrepreneurial history: International Fairs were a real gem in the communist shortage economy, and a source of pride for the citizens. Euro 2012 could have been a mega-event, but it was nothing like the legendary PeWuKa. It was "not done in the Poznanian way" (*zrobione nie po poznańsku*).

The economic critique of the event dominated the discussion about its legacy. Another councillor challenged the assumption that Euro 2012 had enabled the use of European funds and faster completion of some investments, something that supposedly would not have been possible without this stimulus. He also saw it as a proof of the fact that Poland was being given credit: that it had become a serious country in the international arena: "I don't remember anyone among my friends and family being dissatisfied at that time", he said. He acknowledged improvements completed on the occasion of the Euro, but after all, he was sceptical whether we should perceive the event as the necessary condition for new investments:

It is difficult to justify which investments were for Euro because everywhere in Poland, not only in the host cities, a lot has been done in the recent years thanks to the European funds. In Bydgoszcz, in Białystok, in Gorzów, everywhere, not only in the four cities which hosted the championship.... Paradoxically, the only thing which we would have not done in this manner and for that money was the stadium.... I have made some calculations to check if the four cities which got the Euro had more money, for instance, from the "Infrastructure and environment" programme for transportation projects.... And it turned out there was no relation, all the cities, Poznań, Łódź, Kraków, Wrocław, Szczecin,

Bydgoszcz, Gdańsk and one or two more, they all got a more or less equal amount of money. There was no relation between this financial support and the fact that the city was hosting the Euro.

He refers to the argument of "catching up" and becoming a truly European metropolis, but questions the no-alternative rhetoric of the "civilizational jump" on the grounds of economic calculations. The structural funds were not more easily accessible, thanks to the Euro; the councillor questions the power-holders' arguments that the "EU funds would not have waited" and that the tournament enabled them to be used more efficiently. The championship was proof of Poland's post-transformational success and a chance for further changes, but it should definitely not be an explanation for the allocation of European funds in the city and for infrastructural changes financed by those resources.

The oppositional right-wing party also challenged the model of city development in Poznań. A councillor I talked to agreed with the event's advocates that certain investments had brought some benefits to the city, but he also pointed to the fact that because of Euro 2012, Poznań has run up debt. Moreover, because of spending on the tournament, more urgent problems, which the city had been facing for years (such as the lack of social housing), were not solved or even addressed:

It seemed that all host cities would get a huge handicap thanks to Euro 2012, but it turned out that such cities as Cracow or Gdynia, or smaller cities like Toruń, which did not host the event, are developing in a much sustainable way, and were able to solve their problems more efficiently, so we could ask the question what we promoted during Euro if people today live in a city which cannot meet their needs to the extent which cities like Gdynia can. . . . I am making this comparison to show that a city does not need Euro for the citizens to live better, and paradoxically it sometimes might turn out that in some matters Euro is a hindrance, because the money spent on it could have been allocated elsewhere. . . . Maybe citizens do not want to have this high-tech development here, and they are rather concerned with good public transportation and running their own small businesses, not necessarily anything big, rather a bookshop or anything, and about sending their child to a good public school – this is what the city should be investing in, this is how I understand development.

He also noticed that all that was even written down in the city's strategy. The development strategy of the city of Poznań until 2030 (Strategy 2030) was a project from 2009 which specified the local authorities' long-term policy and urban development vision, according to which the Poznań of 2030 should be "a metropolitan city with a strong economy, high quality of life, and relying on knowledge in its development" (Strategy 2013). The strategic goals of the document were grouped in several programmes, but, as the opposition argued, there were no actual long-term plans for achieving the goals listed in the document. My interlocutor did not hide his discontent with the fact that "the mayor admitted at various meetings that a lot of plans listed in this document will not be realized, that those are unrealistic goals which we see as ideal, but which are, in fact, unable to reach. I see it as a completely wrong assumption. All city activities should be based on a long-term plan". Thus, it is long-term planning and strategy, not outer (international) stimuli that should determine city spending.

Moreover, the last councillor also claims to speak in the name of small entrepreneurs and ordinary users of the city, who are more concerned about good quality basic services rather than spectacular projects. He argues that those areas which determine the actual quality of urban life are neglected, and the Euro expenses did not address the real needs of the city's inhabitants. He, therefore, spoke against the elitist character of the event, which neglected the needs of the majority of the citizens. All my interlocutors criticized Euro 2012 for misusing the opportunity: the tournament could have had better results if the promotional branding strategy had been related to the actual situation, i.e. if the entrepreneurial metropolis had been well-managed and had a credible long-term strategy. According to them, the way it was organized served very short-sighted and narrow interests, not those of the community as a whole. As I argued before, Euro 2012 was a clear expression of the entrepreneurial governing model adopted by the city authorities. This ideology and policy were, in turn, legitimized by the entrepreneurial mythology of the city. However, my interviews claim that the discourse behind Euro 2012 was in fact provincial and promoting an old type of modernization, as I was told in the high summer of 2013 by a left-wing local who back then was considering moving out of town. According to him, the rhetoric behind the event did not promote the qualities which are consistent with the self-image of Poznań's citizens, that of diligent workers and skilful entrepreneurs. The realization was hasty and supporting an obsolete type of development. My interlocutor and I ordered cold drinks and sat down in the beer garden located in the post-Prussian part of the city. We started our conversation with exchanging ideas on the Brazilian protests against the World Cup and Summer Olympics, and then moved to discussing the logic behind hosting mega-events in general:

[A]   [Euro 2012 united around] the false idea, around games and the tribal experience of the national community, uncritically supporting the idea of old-style modernization. It's old, because it was a half-baked, uncalculated modernization, without reflection on whether the stadiums should be that big, whether the roads lead in the right directions, whether the railway stations are practical . . . whether this architecture is functional, attractive. It was provincial modernization stemming from our inferiority complexes and from the need to show off.

[Q]   So Euro 2012 was a way to show off?

[A]   Yes, and to make us feel proud of what we are (. . .) But I would rather be proud of good economic relations, of work conditions, of a high quality of life, of everything that the Euro was not promoting. . . . Polish history is the history of spurts, the Euro was yet another uprising in our history, this time not a military one, but one of modernization, although it might sound like a primitive historical analysis. . . . Accession to the EU, the Euro, uprisings. . . . The stimulus might be different, but our history is written from one spurt to another, with times of certain chaos or inertia in between.

Besides the critique of the old type of modernization, an important trope was indicated in this conversation. This is the analogy between the Euro and the historical spurts which are, as I argued before, inconsistent with the local ideal of steady, well-planned development. My interlocutor criticized the rhetoric of the "civilizational jump" as "yet another Polish spurt", a mass mobilization characteristic to the Polish way of "doing politics", which is not focused on steady, sustainable development but depends on short impulses. He ridiculed Euro 2012 by setting it against the history of Polish military uprisings, which, as the reader remembers from the previous chapters, have not been lauded in the former Prussian part of Poland.

According to others, Euro 2012 resembled the celebration of Labour Day in the Polish People's Republic: "everything was subordinated to the Euro, it had priority over anything else – just like the 1st of May back in the old days". This statement discredited the logic behind hosting an expensive football tournament in the city by comparing it to spectacular events organized to the glory of the previous system – the system associated with uneconomic politics and Eastern, slapdash approach to work. The system, which is not praised in entrepreneurial, post-Prussian Poznań. The rhetoric of Euro 2012 as "a civilizational jump" sold a certain model of work and policy, which the opposition forces did not appreciate. Moreover, they associated it with periods in the state's history which are not highly valued in the local imaginarium: poorly prepared and unsuccessful national uprisings, or the national holidays celebrated in the Polish People's Republic. Another interviewee of mine compared the preparation to Euro 2012 to the five-year plans characteristic of the planned economy – not serving the people, but the elites' political goals. This is also why they did not appreciate mayor Grobelny's words, when he openly compared the preparations in the city to how it was decorated before national holidays under Gierek in the 1970s. Subsequently, the project-oriented urban policy was criticized as not embedded in the local system of value, as I was told by yet another opponent of the championship:

> Maybe Euro 2012 was a kick, an impulse for growth, for instance, to build highways, but isn't it paranoia that we don't build them without that impulse? Is should be part of the local government's programme. *Otherwise, it is as if you only cleaned your house for special occasions.*

Such a way of thinking is definitely not compatible with the local tradition of *Ordnung*. Urban activists were even more implacable in their assessments:

> Poznań's strategy is unrealistic. . . . Let's use the metaphor of the family: we sit at the table and create a strategy for the future years, in 20 years we

will have our own house, two cars, I don't know, what else, a bungalow. How will we pay for them? Well, this is not important, it is written there – our own work and bank loans. . . . This is what this city strategy looks like. There is no realistic and credible strategy for making money or fundraising. If Poznań had had this strategy, the city would have known how much money it made and how much it could spend, and maybe it would not have run into debt. This five-year Euro 2012 plan was a spontaneous strategy, and a strategy should not be spontaneous, spending money like there's no tomorrow. . . . *Poznań, which seemed to be a rational city, turned out to be as irrational as others.*

As we can see, the mayor's adherents and opponents referred to the same motif of the local entrepreneurial self-image. Both sides referred to the dichotomy between "economic rationality" and "irrationality". But whereas the power-holders justified their actions – their knowledge and "economic rationality" – by a reference to the competitive logic of the international market ("every city does it", "there is no alternative", "we have to seize the chance"), the opposition pointed out that the *practice* was far from economic and rational. This discrepancy between *neo-liberal* theory and praxis is explicitly addressed in the following passage from my interview with a left-wing activist:

The project to spend billions on activities which were not only dubious, but also uneconomical met with general, irrational applause. It was accepted with acclamation. And this strong supply of resources in the space of five years resulted in an increase in prices on the construction market, a lot of those buildings are defective or unfinished, we have exactly the same situation – maybe not exactly the same, but a similar one – as under Gierek, who was eager to borrow money from Western banks supported by petrodollars. The extensive use of resources had a similar character back then. It is irrational. If it is hammered into people that every action should be based on the profit and loss account, and then you have a stadium for 1 billion zloties and it turns out that this investment is loss-making, then what do you think? Do you think this is rational? Accepting this whole background, which led to the modernization [of the stadium] that will pay off not in a hundred years, not in a hundred and fifty, but in two hundred and fifty years – is it a rational move even from a free-market, neoliberal perspective? Nobody counts 10 extra minutes on their way to work multiplied by the number of working days and the workers, and these hours are worth millions of zloties. Why does nobody analyse it? In any other case, this would be the type of analysis which the government insists on applying! For instance, when they count how many times the city's name was mentioned in the Western press on account of Euro 2012. Each such citation is worth 2000€, multiplied by a thousand times when the name "Poznań" is mentioned...then this rationality is rational, and when we are going in the other direction, then this rationality is not rational.

Another city activist, who claimed to see the positive sides of the event and listed some benefits of the modernization impetus, discussed it extensively during a coffee which we had just a few days after the championship. He talked about how him and his colleagues' views evolved from 2007:

[A]   At the beginning...well, we were glad. We supported the idea, but I think today we would have reacted differently. We are not infallible, and for sure all expenditure on the Euro should be thought over. Not only in Poznań, but in all cities the expenditure on stadiums went through the roof. The question is why. We don't know. Was it because of the deadline that many road investments were more expensive than they would have been had it not been for this timing? There is a discussion whether we, as a nation, really need these events to mobilise us, whether the old Imperial Platform at the railway station would have remained dirty, Głogowska street would have not been widened, the airport would have remained unfinished if we had not had felt the pressure.... And on the other hand, when you look at the balance sheet, how would we have spent the money if there had been no Euro, if the EU funding had been diverted elsewhere. If 300 million had been spent on something else, would not have it been better than three matches and fans visiting the city? There are some benefits when it comes to promotion and tourism.

[Q]   This is the city's main argument when it turns out that we have an adverse balance, these promotional aspects gain crucial importance.

[A]   Well, we surely were spellbound by these opinions on the magic effect of the event. In total, there were eight cities in two countries organising the championships, and does anyone remember today which cities hosted the previous one in Austria and Switzerland? This is where my doubts come from. Of course, we had many visits from journalists who have never heard about this city and wrote a few lines about it, but I am not sure whether the expenditure was not too high. . . . I understand the arguments of the supporters, we got a lot of positive feedback, some new road investments have been started, but there is also the other side of the coin, a lot of money has been wasted, for instance because of this rush to meet the deadlines. Earlier we had this situation when the fast tram to Piątkowo was fouled up, I think it was an administrative mistake, it cost one third more than it would have had it been planned some other time than a year before Euro 2012, and the money could have been spent on something else. The question is *whether we really have to have these national uprisings, whether we have to continue the tradition of national insurrections?* Maybe we do not need them, maybe we do not have to show off? Is it because of our inferiority complex that we always have to be more Popish than the Pope, more western than the West? Do countries with a high quality of life, such as Norway or Sweden, show off anywhere? They do not. If we were to organize such an event again, we would have to analyse all the possible costs.

All the above extracts from my interviews and conversations illustrate the entrepreneurial or industrial strand of the critique. Euro 2012 mobilization, compared with the long history of Polish spurts and insurrections, and communist, uneconomic logic, contrary to the official rhetoric, proved Polish backwardness, because Western countries do not need to "show off". The economic investments, even if some of them are seen as necessary and beneficial to the city's development, were often criticized as inaccurate and too expensive, but first and foremost as not being part of a sustainable, long-term developmental strategy. Although, as I argued before, megaprojects and mega-events are part and parcel of neo-liberalization processes worldwide, the football championship in Poznań was seen by many as a random project. Subordinating all local needs to hosting an expensive event was perceived as a disruption to the urban developmental path. This course could not be applauded in the "bourgeois" Poznań, where people *expected* their government to make rational economic decisions.

Privatizing Profits and Urban Governance, Socializing Costs

Further to the left of this perspective was the interlocutor who not only criticized the execution of the event but also the logic behind it. This was a much more systemic strand of a critique, initially delivered only by a group of activists. For instance, AVE – the PR index used by the city to illustrate the advertising profits of the Euro – was perceived as sort of a symbol of the general politics in the city: concerned with income, not distribution:

> This is virtual money, although we all accustomed ourselves to using it as money of real value. Nobody pays attention to the fact that even economics textbooks use these advertisement indexes not to show a profit, but to show as an equation, which did not mean that such and such company will actually gain this profit from selling, let's say, bricks. If the company was on the stock market, it was not converted into the amount of bricks sold, but also into the company's stock value. And it became more and more complicated, and it applies to the city, too. The value of the company as a producer did not equate to its marketing value, related to the circulation of shares. It produces no additional value and its character is purely speculative. *The shareholders are interested in the company's presence in the press, because it levels up the speculative value of it, but it is separate from real incomes or financial results.* This model was adopted in the city and all *this talk of a knowledge society, of advanced technologies, and of the importance of promotion – all that support the way of looking at a city as a company,* and this is even being explicitly stated. It is being managed as if it were a company, as if it was on some stock market – not if as its value was dependent on the citizens, on what we know and what we do. Do our earnings depend on how many times the name Poznań will be cited in the press?

From this perspective, the power-holders see and manage the city as if it was a company: without public consultations and with its stock value being their main concern. Mayor Grobelny, whose main responsibility is attracting capital to the city and "sucking resources out of" it, as I was told during my research, is seen as a "bookkeeper" or a "pawnbroker in a grand pawnshop":

> Grobelny is killing the city as an entity . . . for instance, by giving privileges to shopping malls over small traders. Shopping malls are like black holes which suck the capital out of a certain place. Euro 2012 was also such a machine to suck out the resources. . . . For instance, take the new tram to Franowo, this is the best example, it is a big investment, in the last ten years there has been a discussion about how much the city needs a new tram route along Naramowicka street, or Ratajczaka street – but no, they built a tram route to the shopping mall, and this is an obvious example of using public money and EU funds to subsidize a private-owned shopping mall! It is not about letting people get to the city, but about letting them get to a peripheral shopping centre, so IKEA can now advertise itself with the slogan "Take a tram to visit us" . . . And this tram route shows how Euro 2012 influenced the development of the city.

This is a more radical and structural critique of the power *status quo*. This position definitely was not the mainstream one, but the idea of a city which should not be run as a company turned to be one of the main motifs in power negotiations in Poznań.

Research proves that hosting mega-events goes hand in hand with change in the governing system. As new policies are more and more dependent on the collaboration between stakeholders and professionals (new elites), they lead to inequality in the access to decision-making and the exclusion of less powerful groups. Swyngedouw et al. call it the "privatization of urban governance" (Swyngedouw et al. 2002: 573) and write that: "the emergence of the NUP [New Urban Policy] rests significantly on the establishment of new forms of intervention at the local level that, to a great extent, constitute a break with traditional forms. Entrepreneurialism is about the public sector running cities in a more business-like manner, in which local government institutions operate like the private sector or are replaced by private-sector-based systems" (573). Others note that "megaproject development today is not a field of what has been called 'honest numbers' . . . [as] project promoters often avoid and violate established practices of good governance, transparency and participation in political and administrative decision-making (. . .) Scandinavians (. . .) have coined a term to describe the lack of accustomed transparency and involvement of civil society in megaproject-related decision-making: 'democratic deficit'" (Flyvbjerg et al. 2003: 5).

Whereas many interviewees criticized Euro 2012 as an uneconomic, badly planned or careless initiative, some openly challenged the tournament as a tool used by the authorities to preserve the status quo of power relations within the city. They criticize the lack of public involvement in the decision-making process. They saw the event as a "natural consequence" of the entrepreneurial logic ruling the city, focused on promotion and the accumulation of capital, and serving the needs of business and of the most affluent and politically influential citizens.

My interlocutors often wondered why politicians did not see the needs of the whole community. They insisted on discussing how to spend each million, "whether it is really worth spending on something, or if it can be moved somewhere else where it is needed more". Many talked about the arrogance of the political and business elites, detached from reality and discussing "not politics, but business", usually only in their narrow circles. But the most anti-systemic opponents questioned the very model of governing, associated with the rise of entrepreneurial cities: the problem which I discussed in the previous chapters. The extracts from my interviews with civil servants, in which they disregarded their opponents as "lacking knowledge" and "irrational", illustrate their beliefs about the role of the governing body. The citizens' political engagement is desired to the extent they are eager to vote and keep the system working. The rule of elites and "experts", joint forces of politicians and business people, was probably best described by a long-term city activist coming from a left-anarchist background. He criticized the uneconomic way the Euro was organized and the authoritarian, centralized way of making decisions about the use of public resources, which led, again, to *profits being privatized and costs socialized*. In his critique, however, he did not stop at criticizing the spending and the elitist way of governing the city. He not only explicitly questions the ideological narrative behind Euro 2012 and unveils the mechanisms which had been used to disregard the oppositional perspective; he argued that appreciating *any* positive changes within the city which resulted from the dominance of this narration hinders us from challenging and changing this dominant discourse:

> Euro 2012 was not just an undertaking, not only a big event, it was a particular ideology. It is an ideology which enabled extensive use of resources while not being in line with [ignoring] other social priorities... it's like communism, like fascism, any ideology which enabled certain groups to make use of vast financial resources.... It was meant to justify the way public money was spent in general.... Moreover, in Poznań the bulk of public money, not European funds, but strictly public money, although I think those two should be analysed together, was spent not even on building a new one, but on modernizing a football stadium. And that clearly proves it is a blatant example of the irrational spending of public money in a centralized way and without any public debate. Of course, not only the local authorities were engaged in the decision-making process, but Poland's governing elites in general, all them. PIS, PO and SLD [Democratic Leftist Alliance, *Sojusz Lewicy Demokratycznej*, a leftist party, by many considered a postcommunist one, but while in power at the beginning of the century implementing *de facto* neoliberal economic policy], all these parties accepted, they bought into this ideology, they united behind the same banner, tinged with a nationalist element, that Poland is yielding social advancement.... Apart from the fact that this is great business for many commercial groups, this is also an ideology, a way to organize public opinion around some problems and issues, and this is the role of sport in general. Of course, sport can be used in many ways, it can be a seedbed of tension, and it may be, as in our case, a way to organize reality, some economic potential... in a particular way, without any unnecessary discussion... for example, without asking whether there is a need for new social housing, for improvements in health care etc. Only a certain type of infrastructure is always financed and it proves that without that type of infrastructure, it is impossible for the whole system to function. But this system cannot function without many subsystems, without the health system, the pension system, social welfare, the education system, but all those are pushed aside.... We can continue to sustain the idea that the truth lies somewhere in the middle, but there is no

objective truth in the middle, the truth lies in breaking with this pattern of thinking and the way the authorities have functioned. We cannot keep on saying that some things were OK. Of course, it is better to have such a railway station than none, although soon it will turn out that this is a complete failure. It is better to have it air-conditioned than not, it is better to have a stadium than not to have one. But the problem lies in the way it affected other aspects of life, the whole city budget. And when it turns out that we've got what we've got but at the expense of other areas of life, then it transpires that the social and economic costs were too high.

Investment plans and promotional arguments do not, he argues, excuse the redirection of public resources and cuts in the budget. This redirection is caused by the fact that the city is not perceived by the authorities as the common good: it is seen as a company which should bring profit to its owners, nothing more. And for the locals, the city' owners turned out to be a too elitist group.

Even local entrepreneurs and businessmen saw Euro 2012 as an example of the city's bad management and planning. But they would rather compare the city to a *badly managed company* than question this resemblance. One of them insisted that the government should learn from people who succeeded in business, because they know "how to count and what should be done to achieve results, and therefore those people would be the best advisers". From this perspective, urban government is seen more as a management board, and the local authorities' main role is to create a business-friendly environment in the city – and the image of such an environment – in order to attract global capital. The tournament's supporters described it as another possibility to speed up certain infrastructural projects and to promote the city on the international market, actions which are both necessary to attract and retain resources in Poznań. The *entrepreneurial opposition*, as I define it, would call it a wasted opportunity or unnecessary expenditure, or enumerate the mistakes which led to the event going well over budget. The economic argument was used by different groups and individuals opposing the official political decisions, and, as I am arguing, it was at least partially backed with reference to the historically constructed, entrepreneurial self-image of Poznań's citizens.

In addition, however, the anarcho-leftist environments together with some urban activists and academics proposed a more systemic argument against Euro 2012 and local politics: that *the city is not a company*, and the citizenship cannot be mistaken for consumption. When the city is governed like a company, the power-holders are interested in business: in profit and in figures. Hence the comparison between the mayor and a "bookkeeper" or a "pawnbroker"; hence the opposition's calls for more democratic procedures in making decisions and discussing undertakings which depend on the use of public resources; and hence the insistence on active and strategic planning of the city's future shape and development rather than solely relying on the free market. It is worth stressing that by "a company", the authors of the slogan understand a neo-liberal model of an investment company, interested in profit (and therefore privatizing and making money on all aspects of urban space, including education and housing), and not being concerned with the well-being of the community. In the Fordist company the well-being of workers allowed them to be active consumers and therefore to buy the products manufactured in the company. When manufacture becomes secondary to the brand, and profit from sales less important than market investments and stock prices (which depends on successful branding), the employee stops being seen by the company as of value (cf. Ouroussoff 2010, Ho 2009).

The mayor's opponents adopted the anti-systemic rhetoric and referred to it in their own critique in a more direct or indirect way, as the councillor who pointed out that the City Hall indeed stopped governing and act like an old, hierarchical company instead:

> The civil servant's role is executive. From the lowest rank to the mayor, they should all carry out the decisions of the City Council, at least that is the legal foundation. This foundation, however, has become rather shaky, as the balance between the executive power and the legislature has changed to the advantage of the executive. I am very critical about it. The mayor elected in direct voting should realize both the people's will and the decisions of the Council. A civil servant should therefore be subordinate to their superiors and indeed be the servant of the citizens.... There are civil servants who are dedicated and serve with a mission, even some working closely with mayor Grobelny, whom I am very critical of...but

in general this team does not share this mission. There are some individuals who are good at what they do, but the whole machinery is rusty, because of being in power for too many years now. *They do not think of themselves as people who govern for the good of citizens, they are rather concerned with figures and organizational matters, tables which are important for a clerk.* And I think it is mostly because they know they depend on the mayor. He has a strong position, been in office for long time now and is supposed to remain there for another while, and this is why the officials are loyal not to the people, but mainly to the mayor. And this is the moment when they cease to fulfil their primary role as civil servants.

The argument that this mode of politics resembles the system of managing a (profit-oriented investment) company was repeated several times during my research. The model of governing the city as it was *owned* by the government and run just for profit was seen as responsible for unfavourable economic decisions regarding the Euro and the stadium:

The authorities still think about this city in old categories. In terms of its transport system, those categories are from the States in the 1950s, so they favour cars and gradually deconstruct the public transportation. On the other hand, the dominant categories are those of post-transformational Poland in the 1990s, where every investment was a good investment and a sign of modernization, of change. It is also a consequence of the particular vision of the city which was adopted at the beginning and is unwilling to change, because that would require them to admit their mistake; and a consequence of some political, social and business links, which we could observe, for instance, when the stadium was built and later, when the agreement with the operator was amended ... and when 2.5 million zloties debt was cancelled and the city gave up its share of the income from selling of the name of the arena.... We lost a few million because the name was sold immediately after signing the annex. And I do not believe that the city did not know about the negotiations, because even the local press wrote about it. ... So, *it's a question of social connections on the hand and the old models from the past on the other hand, which led them to manage the city as if it was a company.*

For many of the critics of urban politics in Poznań and Euro 2012 as its crowning glory, the "civilizational gap" between Poland and the West has its origins in Poland's democratic immaturity rather than in infrastructural deficiencies. This reflects the views of the financial analyst Piotr Kuczyński, who wrote in 2013 that "Poland is an ideological backwater. It's probably only here and in a few other post-communist countries that the elites are so parochial in their economic views. The world experiences a return to Keynesian thinking, economists rediscover the essential role of the state in the economy. We are stuck in the mode of thinking from before the crisis" (Kuczyński 2013). This ideological "backwardness" was often mentioned as one of the main reasons behind the logic and discourse of Euro 2012. When analysing municipal documents and media discourse in his research on Polish entrepreneurship at the end of the first decade of this century, Tadeusz Stryjakiewicz also observed the gradually growing criticism of the general directions of development and urban policy dubbed Grobelism (from the mayor's name Grobelny), which was claimed to involve "maximization of the city's profits at the cost of its residents" (Stryjakiewicz et al. 2010: 54). "Ryszard Grobelny is a president [mayor] of big business and well-to-do Poznanians; for the rest, he sometimes has games to offer", Stryjakiewicz quoted the opponents, who criticized the spatial policy of the city and the degradation of the city centre. He also referred to the scholar and urban activist Andreas Billert's (2009) words, who pointed out that in Poland "urban development is left to the operation of the free market, so that it can make unrestricted use of individual ownership rights... the space of Polish cities has been opened to uncoordinated investments first and foremost satisfying the interests of the investors or a narrow group of users.... Since they do not follow from a consistent conception of the city's integrated development, those investments do not ensure Poznan a modern type of development" (Stryjakiewicz et al. 2010: 51–5). What they ensured in the case of Euro 2012 was redirecting scarce urban resources from wider social needs into funding a certain type of infrastructure and business, i.e. privatizing profits and socializing costs – and all that without making use of the democratic instruments of public consultation. For many critics of the event that was a sign of parochialism of the local elites, who seemed to got stuck in the 1990s. Not every business opportunity is good, and focusing only on financial income is a short-sighted politics. Power-holders should not rely only on market fluctuations and business opportunities. They should actively participate in shaping the city's profile and image, and the distribution of resources. Otherwise, they lose control over how the city develops and whether it in fact creates a good climate for investment. In other words, the city should be an important player in local politics. If it steps down, it leaves room for random investments and short-term projects aimed at individual profit rather than at the common good of urban society:

> The local government has a great impact on how the city develops: it gives permission for erecting new buildings, and the large number of the shopping malls in the city is a consequence of the land management we have. If we decide not to have new shopping malls but, let's say, more swimming pools, then I understand we are ready to go for it, even whether we have an investor or not – now we rather expect that in exchange for the permission to build another shopping centre, an investor will pay for new traffic lights or build a pedestrian crossing. But the game is not worth the candle, this style of politics kills the city.... This is all because at the beginning of their term of office the politicians adopted the model which treats a city as an enterprise. *To manage an "enterprise city" is to run it like a business, when you are only concerned with income and outcome.* But a city has whole areas of life where this simple calculation of profits and losses does not apply. When we wanted to be a "city of culture", they laughed at us, because this would not suit their vision of an enterprise. Take this simple example, we plan a new housing development and theoretically, the most profitable thing would be to build the narrowest streets possible and the highest buildings, to get the most out of every square metre. But the quality of life would then drop and soon people living there would move elsewhere, so we would get more money in a short time but then we will lose when it turns out that in a different city they thought about a park or a green space nearby.

This comparison of a city with a company also applies to the hierarchical relation within the municipal structures. I have already quoted councillors who explained local politics by referring to the background of the civil servants, the historical context of the time when they came to office, and to the relations between the top officials and lower-ranking officials. A city activist who worked in the town hall for a few months in the past and could not stand the atmosphere of the place recalled that in the 1990s Poznań experienced a real investment boom, but then the authorities overslept and the years of the doldrums came. According to him, the appearance of the first urban movements and associations was an answer to the stagnation among the authorities and power-holders, who are "fanatics of the old theories". There is no investment strategy which would have the sustainable development of the whole city as its goal: there are only particular business interests. There is a need for good governance, for politics devoted to the city, and not just interested in political gain: "They all think, in a strange and fanatical way, that they are always right, that they are the best, and that the citizens are a problem for them, and NGOs are the biggest one, they are their cosmic enemy. I do not understand this attitude". The urban activists point out that the power-holders in the city are utterly detached from reality:

> We wanted to invite the mayor's deputy for a short walk in the city, make him wait two minutes for a green light and use an underground passage – he is a great supporter of those, so is the director of the Municipal Roads – while carrying a bag or pushing a pram, make him wait for a delayed tram, they do not know and see it, and even if they do, they pretend this is not a problem.... And those people are paid from our taxes. I told it once to one civil servant and he was indignant, he did not want to talk to me. But this is a fact, and I do not understand why they have no shame.... When people get together and start to fight for something, a civil servant should come and check what they want, talk with them. And there is no dialogue, as if they were afraid of change or as if they had no consciousness.... In Poznań there is this role-model mayor, Cyryl Ratajski, "father of PeWuKa", who everyday went to the city and observed, and saw its problems.... If a mayor is taken everywhere by car ... and I do not understand why he must use a company car, if he wants, let him drive his own, I am so angry ... and I wish he only used a bus. It would be so much easier for him, if he were with the people. This is the problem, this detachment from reality. Ok, let him live in the suburbs, this is not ideal, but he should be present in this space, it really pisses me off when he gets on the tram before elections and meets with people.... For God's sake, *is he a tsar?* It should be obvious that this is not any favour, he gets

money from the people, this is the gist of it, he should listen to people who pay taxes, because they pay him for listening to them and deal with what bothers them. There must be a dialogue between him and them. But maybe it is better to listen to some lobby groups rather than to ordinary citizens? Maybe this the mystery of power and money?

The need for a government concerned with local matters, actively engaged in shaping the architectural and social space of the city, drawing good inspiration from the West, not mimicking bad and old examples – this is what united different circles against mayor Grobelny after Euro 2012, the "crowning achievement" of his governance.

The Betrayal of the Middle Class

The crux of the conflict between the pro-Euro forces and their opponents is the discrepancy between the visions of the city's development. As I have been arguing here, the adherents referred to "the historically developed assets of Poznań: entrepreneurship and high work standards" (PWC 2011: 11, cf. PWC 2007), but the opposition challenged the legitimacy of their decisions by invoking the very same values: that of economic rationality, development and modernization, and high quality of work. The anti-Euro (and simultaneously anti-governmental) forces criticized the rapid and hasty manner in which the tournament was organized, although on different grounds. For many, it was the proof of the authorities' lack of business expertise. For some, it proved the power-holders' inability to understand that the city is *something more than just business* and should be governed through bigger engagement in public affairs and broader public consultations. But differences among critics notwithstanding, they had a lot in common.

For most of them, the idea that hosting sport mega-event was a chance for civilization (*modernization*) jump was far-fetched – and for many reasons. "What", they asked, "if we had not had the Euro, these infrastructural projects would not have been realized? We would not have built airports and railway stations? Especially in Poznań, this rhetoric that the Euro equals modernization and the lack of the Euro equals the lack of modernization could not work". When Donald Tusk started talking about organizing the Winter Olympics in Cracow in 2022, they did not hide their astonishment. "It is unbelievable for me", told me a friend, "because we are expected to pay extra money to the infrastructure which would have been built anyway, but then it would not have been a huge project, but ordinary life: we build a new road, it is not seen as a huge task, and there is no pressure that we have to finish it on time, otherwise the West will say we are not able to do anything". It does resemble the picture of the nineteenth century Poznań, which was focused on steady development, not spurts and overinvested projects.

For this group, the decision to not host the event would have been a real proof of the country's (and city's) advancement. The way Euro 2012 was introduced and hosted in Poland proved precisely an opposite: it was evidence of the lack of maturity. It is true that the West and the East remain the significant Others for those who criticize the official governmental and local rhetoric of the civilization leap. The key difference between the dominant and the dominated discourse during my research was the reason for Polish civilizational backwardness. For the power-holders it was a matter of the lack of the necessary infrastructure and of global promotion, which could attract capital to the city. For many of their opponents, Poland suffers mostly because of the backwardness of its power-holders, who rather than support democratic institutions (such as public consultation, referenda, open discussion, public information) and learn from western countries' experience (which, in the opinion of the opposition, is more concerned with culture and the everyday use of the city by its inhabitants), run the city as it was their company. The uneconomic actions of the local elites cannot create a genuinely entrepreneurial atmosphere in the city. As such, they could not be beneficial to the whole community but only to the narrow elitist group of politicians and allied business, who "knew-how" to make a good use of hosting the event in Poznań.

The only partially successful part of the event was its promotional aspect. My interlocutors were not hyper-enthusiastic about it but saw some positives in the fact that the city was described and advertised in the international media. Despite this, they would rather see the city promoting through things different than sport. As a young student and a city activist told me before Euro 2012, a disproportionate amount of money is spent on expensive sports infrastructure rather than on the sustainable development of the city:

> In my opinion, Euro is primarily for UEFA, for the sponsors who make money from it and for the people who may benefit from the event. And for the politicians who see it as a chance to promote their country. And it is difficult to say whether the Euro in Portugal or Austria indeed promoted those countries. . . . Maybe they did, but I still think that the money spent on the event is incommensurable; yes, you can promote a country through sport, but I reckon more important is financing and building through the method of small steps – it is better to build a good infrastructure with bicycle paths and public transportation rather than a billion-dollar stadium.

He declares to be a frequent visitor to Berlin and considers it a benchmark for modern cities, also in terms of infrastructural development. He highlighted the example of Berlin Brandenburg International Airport as illustrating a different "culture" of construction: well-planned, sustainable and carefully prepared before the opening. We talked in May 2012, a few days before Euro, and his praise of the airport is particularly interesting, considering that Berlin's new airport was later seen as one of the biggest construction failures in Germany, and a nail in the coffin of mayor Klaus Wowereit (Berlin Mayor to Resign After Criticism 2014). Despite the budgetary problems experienced by the German capital, it is worth mentioning that for the critics of the tournament and local politics in Poznań, there are examples to follow not only in Berlin but also in smaller German cities, such as the already mentioned Dresden or Leipzig. He and other interlocutors put great emphasis on promoting the city through culture. Culture is linked with innovation and knowledge, and it is through culture not sport that we can compete with other Western cities: "Because this is the choice we have, we will either be a country of workmen and labourers, who work on someone else's projects, or a country with creative people who make things on their own. When we support sport, we support short-lived entertainment instead of development". Supporting sport is seen as short-sighted entertainment rather than development.

A small entrepreneur told me that Poznań cannot afford events like the Euro, and that rather than organizing a wedding for a daughter for 200 guests and then paying loans till the end of life, he would rather have a small ceremony and spend the saved money on his grandchildren's education. He criticized the spending on the stadium and the event and doubted whether they would pay off at all. He was also very critical of the theatrical character of Polish football, and how uprooted it is from locality and how disproportionate the players' earnings are; and, like many of my interlocutors, considered football to be a quite vulgar entertainment, in contrast to high culture: "It is like the difference between vodka and a fancy cocktail", he told me. He also noticed that today football divides rather than unites people: Euro 2012 and life around the stadium led to a degree of opposition among citizens. The stadium is a natural consequence of the beliefs of people who are in the governing apparatus in other Polish cities, not just in Poznań. On many occasions I have been told that the VIP room at the city stadium is a new political salon, which tells us a lot about the tastes of the political and business elites. Their politics, according to this entrepreneur, was leading to the situation where "Poznań becomes something like a Brazilian city, with a lot of poverty and a small group of princes, who meet for fun and business at the city stadium".

For those critics, civilizational advancement would mean investing in culture and the democratization of public life, or, in other words, drawing on the Western (German) experience of urban politics. It is evident that the decisions made by the current city authorities differ from their perception of development and modernity.

Above all, all my interviewees who are in opposition to mayor Grobelny spoke in the name of groups which, in their opinion, were excluded from both the process of decision-making and getting their slice of the cake after the tournament: those who live outside the revamped parts of the city, not using new airports and entertainment facilities, suffering from budgetary cuts on public services and less prioritized investments. Even those business representatives who regretted that the city is a badly managed company advocated for those who, contrary to expectations, did not benefit from hosting the tournament. In fact, many of my interlocutors saw the ongoing debate as a conflict between two different forces, offering two different models of urban development. As I was told by one of my interviewees, "According to one of those models, the city is for everyone, no matter how rich you are; according to another, your income defines your access to better or worse parts of the city". This corresponds with Saskia Sassen's differentiation between two groups in the city (1996): those who advocate an alliance with big business and making money, and those who stand up for poor people.

Most city activists are in fact aware that Euro 2012 was not a coincidence but had a strategic meaning for local urban politics. This is probably one of the major differences between the opposition forces within the City Council, most of whom initially saw Euro 2012 as a great chance for the city, followed by some business circles questioning the uneconomic spending during the tournament, and a lot of the city activists who openly criticized the logic which decided on hosting the event in the city and in the country. Of course, the demarcation line between those groups, one challenging the performance and the other additionally the ideology (as it was called in some of my interviews), is not straight. Some councillors openly referred to the neo-liberal doctrine which dominates in power-holders' circles in the city; some city activists admitted they saw positive aspects in hosting the tournament. What all those four groups shared is the reference they make to the Poznań's entrepreneurial *ethos* – as well as to historical periods and characteristics which are not valued in the local imaginarium.

One of the fiercest critics of the mayor's politics was not surprised that some of the people saw Euro 2012 as evidence that Poznań was on the right track to becoming a truly European metropolis and Poland's second city, but himself perceived it more as a burden than an opportunity. He insisted on seeing these views as mirroring the government's neo-liberal way of thinking about the city:

> Euro 2012 determined the perspective of a semi five-year plan in the sense of civilizational development. . . . The decision that Poland would host Euro was made in 2007, and in 2006 Grobelny was elected mayor of the

city in a public election for the second time. And in the city at that time there was a peak of optimism, it might sound like a slogan, but it was the peak of the neoliberal development of the city. This meant that big capital was flowing into the city, we put some money in, the city gets wealthier, becomes more attractive, people want to visit it, we have Termy etc. And that was a lie from the very beginning, and the Euro was a keystone of this rhetoric, it was to direct the spending of money. When we look at the city's debt, which today amounts to about 2 billion zloties, we see that two-thirds of it, or even three-quarters are related to Euro 2012.... In my opinion, Poznań was not able not to aspire to the Euro once the decision to grant the event to Poland was made, and that was a disaster.... It was a dramatic situation and maybe there was no chance to avoid it, in any political configuration. But I am deeply convinced that it does not serve the development of the city. We must say it honestly, we stepped into the shit and we must do whatever possible not to go deeper, but to wash it off. Because even in this situation, we could have optimized the expenditures, we did not have to build such a huge stadium. And they do something completely opposite.

This critical stand defines Euro 2012 as a result of a certain vision of the city, a certain mode of governing represented by mayor Grobelny. It was the neo-liberal vision of economic development which justified the organization of the event, and it was the very same logic which justified spending public money without a long-term business plan. This is what Harvey had in mind when he wrote about the discrepancy between neo-liberal theory and practice (Harvey 1989; cf. Polanyi 2001 [1944]). It is the vision of profit which decided on the practice and reigned in the political salons: profit for a certain class, which is also the only bene-ficiary of events such as Euro 2012, able to enjoy the "chocolate parts of the city" revamped before the tournament. This individualist, market-oriented rhetoric of the neo-liberal authorities initially met with sym-pathy in Poznań, proud of its entrepreneurial ethos, but the uneconomic management of public money during Euro 2012 put this relation to the test.

Opposition forces, and later the slowly growing number of other citizens, realized that this policy serves the particular interests of certain individuals and groups, and is very unfavourable to the regular user of public space and public services. And those regular users referred to the middle-class ethos of their city understood in the Weberian sense: associated with diligence and accumulating wealth, yet living frugally and not consuming excessively. It was explicitly expressed by one of the city activists when we discussed the goals of the local politics:

> We go back to the question of whether Grobelny represents the middle class. No. If he represented the middle class, he would build houses for families, or let people build them, but he does not do it. He is generally interested in big financial flows and plucking some of them. This is why he came up with this second Olympics [YOG], this is how Euro 2012 worked. There was no business plan there and it is obvious that events like those are always loss-making.

The ethos of entrepreneurship, of thriftiness, of German-like affection for *Ordnung* – those are the endangered virtues of the middle class, which are a constituent part of the local identity. Mayor Grobelny, as part of the system, did not serve the interests of the people who appreciated those values:

> For years Grobelny has pursued politics of the particular interests of some sort of oligarchy. This accusation really hurt Civic Platform in Poznań: that Grobelny and his team betrayed the middle class in Poznań, they were interested in big business and it is clearly visible when you look at their priorities; all decisions are favourable to big business, not small or medium-sized ones. A clear example of this are the shopping malls and supermarkets, how they ruin small businesses and service providers, Św. Marcin and Głogowska are practically ghost streets today. And this is just an example, take a look at what happens in the housing industry and how people flee the city centre for the estates built by developers in the suburbs.

This is not a late capitalism understanding of the middle class which was promoted in the post-transformational reality of the city, while being linked with the local ethos of resourcefulness. Yet the local understanding of middle class – and its interests – is rooted in the ethics developed in the Prussian and interwar Poznań, which I described above. It has been articulated in Poznań for years, influencing people's expectations

POZnan*

* Miasto know-how

Fig. 4.1   The official logo of Poznań, "the city of know-how"

and self-image and deciding on the success of some social and political projects, and the failure of others (Figs. 4.1 and 4.2).

In order to avoid drawing a simplifying dichotomous picture of the power relations in Poznań, we must differentiate between various groups which emerged during the struggles over the dominant modernist discourse in the city. They are neither clear-cut nor static categories, but in

Fig. 4.2   A stencil saying "Poznań is not a company". The official city star was replaced by a five-pointed symbol of communism, and the official blue colour – by red (photo by the author)

the discussion on the future politics and development of the city, a few positions and interest groups can be singled out. I have tried to show some discrepancies between various arguments against the way Euro 2012 was organized in the city, as well as different standpoints and visions behind them; I will now scrutinize them and juxtapose them with the until recently dominant rhetoric represented by mayor Grobelny and his adherents.

The football tournament and the discussion around it revealed certain tensions in local politics and brought forth arguments against the system which had remained unquestioned for decades following the transformation in 1989. The main argument in this debate, used by all groups engaged in the discussion, was a reference to the entrepreneurial mythopraxis of the local community. Euro 2012 led to the introduction of the initially leftist–anarchist slogan, "the city is not a company", and thus to a broad discussion. As a result of it, the legitimacy of the power-holders in Poznań and their decisions was threatened and subsequently denied.

The mayor of the city, the civil servants working in the town hall and several bodies engaged in organizing the Euro represented the interests of the old, post-transformational elites; those interests were also expressed by the united national political circles before and during the championship. They all described Euro 2012 as a great "civilizational jump", or a chance for one, and indeed saw it as a giant leap in the Polish modernization process. Large-scale infrastructural and revamping projects in the city were directly linked with the opportunity of hosting an international sports mega-event: the tournament was seen as a kick which helped speed up necessary investments and turn the city into a truly European location accessible through a functional airport, new railway station and road transport routes. However imperfect or over-priced those infrastructural projects were – and some of them remained unfinished three years after the first whistle – they are a qualitative change: the city enjoys better connections, especially with its western neighbours, and benefited from new investments, although the choice of those might be criticized as unjustified. Moreover, those projects derived from, and at the same time sustained the entrepreneurial promotional strategy, which the peripheral city adopted in order to compete for global capital. This strategy worked for many who believed in the free market and private initiative as solutions to the post-socialist backlog of the country and argued that neither Poznań nor the country has any alternative if they want to be treated as a serious player on the international economic scene. Euro 2012 was the crowning event in the post-transformational history of the city. It opened up possibilities for both private business and for turning the city into an even more business-friendly, accessible investment location. As such, it cannot be seen as a random event that just happened in a particular location, but more as a part of a long-term, deliberate urban strategy, and a "promotional vehicle" of a certain, neo-liberal way of thinking about the city.

Yet this strategy, legitimized by a reference both to the global conditions ("there is no alternative") and to the merchant history of the city, was heavily criticized precisely on the occasion of the Euro. The first sort of criticism came somehow from the within of this elite group. Some members of the political (including city councillors) and business elites of the city questioned the rhetoric and strategy implemented by the local government as uneconomic and non-entrepreneurial. This group saw the city as a badly managed company and the authorities as abusing the local tradition of diligence, *Ordnung* and careful business planning. Certain investments were criticized as ill-considered and overpaid, and the supposed benefits of hosting the tournament as insignificant when compared to the costs. My interlocutors recommended that the authorities learn from people who had actually succeeded in business and knew how to make money. According to them, by organizing the championship in a hasty way, the power-holders betrayed the local value system, the *imaginarium*, which acclaims long-term, profitable initiatives. Their critique could be seen as in line with that of Bob Jessop's, who differentiated between cities which are concerned with creating a truly attractive business environment and those which are focused solely on creating the image of an entrepreneurial location. This group also claimed to speak in the name of the general public, who, they argued, because of the wrong, short-sighted political decisions, was deprived of the possibility of developing their entrepreneurial skills and could not enjoy the kind of urban growth which would be consistent with their self-image. I would argue that their arguments were of crucial significance during the discussion on urban politics in Poznań, precisely because they referred to the middle-class entrepreneurial tradition of the place, shared by the majority of citizens and described in the previous chapters.

However, in the final round against mayor Grobelny and his team, these arguments were to a great extent supported by the more radical, leftist critique, coming from the circles of urban activists and intellectuals (such as journalists or academics). This standpoint calls for a systemic change, not only for a reform of the existing one. Its adherents argue that the city is not a company, and should not be governed as such: it should not be interested only in profit, but rather in the well-being and sustainable future of all city inhabitants. They also claim to speak in the name of the underprivileged and unrepresented citizens, and fight the common rhetoric of the Euro as a chance for everyone with a business idea. From their perspective, the tournament sucked and diverted scarce city resources from the burning social needs to the areas where only well-off citizens could benefit, i.e. commerce and leisure. Even if they acclaimed the investments in the city, they questioned them as deriving from a specific, neo-liberal vision of the city. This vision, they argued, is not even business-oriented: it is oriented towards big business only and not concerned with the needs of small local entrepreneurs, as shown by the example of the consecutively built shopping malls, which push small traders out of the market. They saw Euro 2012 as part of the same logic which transforms the authorities from political actors, actively shaping the character and the future of the city, into bookkeepers concentrating solely on figures and Excel sheets. This form of politics, they demonstrated, led to the privatization of profits and socializing of costs. As such it was harmful to the city and to the majority of its inhabitants, especially those who rely on well-functioning public services and cannot afford regular visits to new leisure centres. This group would be particularly concerned with discussing the global problems of capitalism and its local, post-transformational version. When they referred to the local *articulated tradition* of entrepreneurialism, they did so to show that the urban politics did not meet the citizens' needs. And those needs would be *Ordnung*, appreciation of their economic activity and resourcefulness, and rational economy of public resources. Of course, like any of the groups discussed above, it is not homogenous, but it might be singled out due to its anti-systemic character. The key motto of this type of critique, "the city is not a company", was sometimes also used by the representatives of the entrepreneurial strand of the anti-governmental opposition: it helped them position themselves against the power-holders, who claimed to "know better" than anyone else.

The fourth group in these negotiations over urban politics and future visions for the city was the majority of the citizens, who did not take the floor in public debates and media. The government's opponents claimed to speak in their name, and even if they had not at the very beginning, they definitely influenced their opinions and voting preferences, as proved by the local elections in autumn 2014.

5

Conclusions. Shifting Meanings, New Knowledge Production

My fieldwork proved that Euro 2012 was not only the hallmark but also the crowning glory of the *modernization* and *entrepreneurial* strategy of the city of Poznań. The tournament was used by the elites to promote the image of the city as a business-friendly, European location while referring to the commercial history of Poznań and the entrepreneurial self-image of its citizens. Ryszard Grobelny compared himself with the legendary mayor of the city from the interwar period, Cyryl Ratajski. The event was often set against the legendary exhibition of Ratajski's epoch, a major undertaking in the liberated city and the moment of a great surge in investment, which began the era of hosting international fairs in Poznań, linking it with the capitalist West, even during the Cold War. In their efforts to present themselves as great hosts with strong organizational and entrepreneurial skills, the authorities refer to the local tradition of scrupulous, "organic work" and the experience in international trade and business.

As I tried to show, and what was noted by some of my interlocutors, Euro 2012 was not an *ad hoc* initiative, an accident in an otherwise consistent urban development strategy. On the contrary, it was an

© The Author(s) 2017   **119**
M.Z. Kowalska, *Urban Politics of a Sporting Mega Event*,
Football Research in an Enlarged Europe,
DOI 10.1007/978-3-319-52105-3_5

unequivocal expression of neoliberal ideology and entrepreneurial policies, which initially, due to the economic and systemic transformation after 1989, were endorsed by the local community. The market-oriented strategy suited this city, which takes pride in its thrift and flair for business, "renowned for generations". For 25 years after the transformation, but especially after the 16-year reign of Mayor Grobelny and his team, this governing model, backed by the ideology of the free market and focused on attracting outer capital to the city, prospered well. The authorities supported investors of any kind (for instance, through tax allowances – UEFA being no exception here – and through municipal programmes and offices providing companies with orientation in legal and administrative matters) and were devoted to create an image of Poznań as a business-friendly metropolis. This variety of politics was at the same time complemented and justified by the narrative of a resourceful and proactive *middle class*. The beneficiaries of this system were those who knew how to make use of their chance and do business, those who "know-how" to "play the lottery".

But, as I also wrote elsewhere (Kowalska 2014), rather than consolidating the existing power relations, Euro 2012 actually reinforced the discussion on the general course of Poland's economic and social development and the shape of its democracy. For years in favour of big business and growth-oriented, entrepreneurial urban strategies left many cities drained of resources and indebted. Euro 2012 was part of the logic which enabled taxpayers' money to be redirected from financing public services to sponsoring a certain type of infrastructure and promotion. As such, it led to privatization of any possible profits from hosting the event and the socialization of its costs.

I examined how a local tradition was adopted by a promotional campaign aiming at depicting Poznań as a "world-class city", welcoming big international capital and foreign tourists, whose visits were supposed to bring revenue to private business and the public purse (and who were also expected to be potential investors in the region). This campaign, therefore, was addressed to the well-off visitor, and although it spoke about increasing the "quality of life" and the well-being of all inhabitants of Poznań, who should benefit from infrastructural investment in the city, it saw them more as customers than citizens. Those who could afford to make use of the new infrastructure and knew how to make money during the championship were the real winners of the tournament. According to the authorities, they also personified the local virtues of enterprise.

Yet, as part of the "neoliberal rescaling project", which, according to Glick Schiller and Çağlar, "triggers social processes, social resistance, and new forms of power struggles and articulation of interests among the existing social groups" (Glick Schiller and Çağlar 2011c: 80), Euro 2012 exposed the premises of the dominant public discourse, which could have been beneficial for individuals, but were unfavourable to the community as a whole. The local policies and actions, including organization of the event, were challenged by the opposition forces as being elitist, short-sighted and, ironically, uneconomic. Euro 2012, although both part of and the consequence of the urban strategy developed in the city for decades, simply turned out to be a bridge too far.

Businessmen and entrepreneurs complained that the event did not bring them the expected benefits (excluding companies directly involved in the Euro infrastructural projects). Together with opposition city councillors, they argued that the city proved to be a badly managed "rusty machinery". Some of them proposed that the power-holders should cooperate more closely with advisors who had enjoyed success and indeed knew how to do business. Maintaining capital accumulation, administering a business-friendly climate and image and attempting to use strategies working to good effect elsewhere are not sufficient for the city to be considered entrepreneurial. What matters in this competition is genuine innovation: "supply of relevant knowledge and organizational intelligence rather than capital; . . . shaping the institutional context in which firms operate rather than providing subsidies; . . . organizing place-specific advantages rather than an abstract space of flows; and . . . the (re-)territorialization of activities rather than their emancipation from spatial and temporal constraints" (Jessop 2013 [1998]). This last point is particularly interesting in our discussion, because the success of the entrepreneurial strategy also depends on its embodiment in the local context. "Emphasiz[ing] instead the 'animal spirits' of gifted individuals or equally inspired corporations" (Jessop 2013 [1998]) does not translate into long-term success. The strategy chosen by the authorities, which they themselves described as being backed by beliefs in a rising tide that lifts all boats and in a market where everybody can win, if only "know-how", was debunked as uneconomic, ineffective and damaging to the city. Sport was deemed short-sighted entertainment rather than a serious investment in development and utilizing local potential. Crucial infrastructural investments were criticized as badly planned and managed, often of doubtful architectural and functional merit, resulting from the power-holders' obsolete attitude towards modernization. The promotional campaign, revolving around the motifs of a "civilizational jump" and becoming a European "metropolis", was questioned as self-orientalizing, and above all, as expensive and unnecessary.

More importantly, however, and that was the second strand of the critique, people in Poznań started to comprehend that what is good for big business is not necessarily good for the community. After the public resources were "sucked" from other areas to support the Euro project, the city started lacking money for services which determined its standing as clean, well organized and tidy. Because of the cuts in the budgets for public transportation and municipal roads, street lighting and cleaning, the streets in the city centre were covered either in snow, or in dirt, and remained pitch-dark before dawn and well after dusk. Teachers from public nurseries and kindergartens continued to live on low salaries, whereas parents paid more for their children' day care. Acknowledging the fact that the money was spent on Euro 2012 rather than on the everyday needs of the community, and that the biggest beneficiaries of the tournament do not rely upon an efficient public schooling and transportation system led to concern being voiced about the direction in which the city is developing.

For the most radical opponents, the modernization process in Polish cities is doubly flawed. Firstly, there is a discrepancy between the elites' vision and reality: in Poznań, officials tried to promote the city as a bustling European metropolis, whereas it is a medium-sized and rather peripheral "town" with a slow pace of life. However, it used to be distinguished by its *Ordnung* and thrift. Yet the elites' ambitions have put those virtues in danger. Secondly, and this is an even more important strand of this critique, the whole discussion on investment as proof of Poland's "civilizational jump" in fact diverts attention away from more vital problems, such as the goals of the modernization process in Poland. Euro 2012 exposed all the post-transformational problems not only in Poznań but also in the country as a whole. Some of my interlocutors, like the following, supporting the "Bread Instead of Games" initiative, saw the problem in a broad perspective:

> If you go to the railway station and see the plans of the new station and the shopping mall, a futuristic building of the 21st century, and then you compare these plans and photos with the view of the station from Głogowska street, you will notice a lot of huge air conditioners on the roof, marring this view and which you could not find on the plans; because of these air conditioners, this view is anything but futuristic. It is not designed as in the West, where the air conditioners would not have been visible.... I am not sure, but I do not think they will be removed in the future. This makes the whole landscape, with the beautiful old building of Dworzec Zachodni, damaged, and this object looks like a giant heap of scrap, not a futuristic design. So even on this futuristic level, we must admit that the "know-how city" narrative, the city of high technology, where these air conditioners should be hidden, is not appropriate...I do not think that everything should be perfect, but the problem is that we have a dissonance between visions and the reality of a parochial city in a provincial country. And being parochial is fine, why can't we draw strength from what is a benefit, that we do not have to cope with some conurbation problems.... And the question of the transformation of the Polish cities, not only Poznań, 25 years after the political transition, is a question of whether we have a new idea how to manage public resources, how to manage the cities. Not whether we know how to build, let's say, a venue in the shape of a sphere, completely transparent and using no energy, but *the question is who decides about that and who is it for, and what is it for.*

This is a particularly complex critique of the ongoing type of modernization in Poland: supporting short-term projects, random investments, ignoring the need for systemic change and planning. The extract exemplifies the concerns raised about the long-term politics in the community. What kind of society do we want? Should the government only enable private initiatives to prosper in the city? Is there any need for a society at all, or can we only speak of "individual men and women", as Margaret Thatcher was suggesting? Until recently, those questions were not even raised in Poznań. The same interviewee recalled how alternative visions and niche ideas of governance and administering public money were disregarded by the elites, which helped the power-holders to present their views and decisions as rational and a matter of natural choice: "This is how ideology works", he said, "different views are discredited as irrational, populist, or whatever". Aware of the leading role of Gramsci's "intellectuals" in securing the hegemonic status quo, he notices that "People allow some things to happen because they are in a structurally worse position than the power-holders. They are not allowed to be heard".

Many opponents of the championship and Mayor Grobelny saw power as serving the interests of the most affluent and influential citizens, and not taking into account the needs of other social groups. One of the urban activists gave me an example of the public day-care system and argued that 10 or 20% of women are able to cope without public services, and they would not be interested in developing this institution; and those, he argued, would be the families of political and business elites in the city who decide on local spending. The remaining 80–90% cannot afford private nanny or babysitter, which means they are dependent upon the well-functioning public schooling. They would be the losers of shuffling public money. The opposition tried to explain why the elites stick to free market ideology and the belief in private initiative as the key to modernization and development, and refuse to see excluded members of society as the victims of their own actions:

> Let's maybe put it differently: the city is not active on the housing market or elsewhere, it takes no initiative, because it believes in the self-regulation of the market. . . . This is still the way or the mode of thinking from the nineties, those people believe in the same things as in the nineties, but maybe it is also because when the head of an institution holds particular views . . . his subordinates share his opinions . . . ? This is just my feeling, but yes, especially in the middle-aged generation people are still like that. This is the generation which gained a lot thanks to the changes in the 90s and therefore . . . somehow, it is impossible to question the model which

gave them personal success, affluence and social status, it would probably be difficult for them to separate from it or look at this system or ideology in a critical way.

The system works for those who thrived under the economic and social conditions of the post-transformational years. Euro 2012, as its hallmark event, exposed the inequalities between the beneficiaries and losers, and resulted in a discussion about the need for qualitative change. Left-wing circles proposed a general vision of a city which is friendly not only to the well-off citizens – or consumers – and big business but also to the community as a whole. One of my respondents was sure that after the Euro, people eventually realized that power does not serve their interests, but only that of the richest'. He compared Grobelny's politics to that of Edward Gierek back in the 1970s and made an interesting comment about how the elites – not only those in Poznań – are detached from reality. We talked in the autumn after the tournament, two years before the local elections (and three before the parliamentary elections which radically changed the political scene in the country):

I am not sure if [Grobelny] was stupid or arrogant, or both . . . but they decided not to worry about anything and steal as much as possible during their last term, and for instance they made those cuts on lighting and the streets are dark in the morning, and this is probably because they did not notice that many people leave for work earlier than 8 or 7 a.m. They are detached from reality. And the same happened with Solidarność, Gierek spent all the money and it was over, and now we have the same situation, you have a boom and then a crisis, and a social movement which responds to it. . . . And Warsaw too is detached from reality. People at the top of "Gazeta Wyborcza" do not leave left-bank Warsaw and they still support Balcerowicz. It is nice and pretty in Warsaw, so what's a big deal? But no big social movement started in Warsaw. They are detached from reality and they have too much to lose. *We have to make the change.*

Many of my interlocutors noticed some changes in the official discourse, introduced as an answer to concerns raised by the public, who were becoming more socially engaged. However, they argued that employing the opposition's arguments in the official rhetoric was just another attempt to defend the status quo:

> I think that the city understands [the situation] to some extent and that is why it absorbed some of these concepts, like, participatory budgeting. But all that is so insincere.... I recently talked with someone about the fact that the less democracy we have, the more centralised the power is – and the less legitimized it becomes. Our authorities have no legitimacy, I mean, they have formal legitimacy, because the elections were not rigged, but only 16% of all those eligible voted for the Council, and only 24% for the mayor. They do not have social legitimacy. And the less legitimacy those in power have, the more megalomaniac and punctual are the investments financed with the public money are – the more they talk about public consultation. Nobody remembers this today, but the term "public consultation" was introduced not after 1989, but in the late 70s, in the days of the first Solidarity. It proves that this face-lift will not solve any problems and we have to rethink the ways we understand and manage the city. And for now, the screen has frozen.

This passage brings me to discuss the long-term results of the change. As I wrote in the Preface and as I explained in the body of this book, the citizens of Poznań showed its mayor a red card after the football tournament, whose organization, course and effects proved to be inconsistent with the local system of values and their *expectations, sentiments and beliefs* (Holmes 2014), which are both shaped by and shapers of this system (i.e. *they determine the process of articulation of the local tradition*). The mayor was criticized as being "just a clerk who designs the city through virtual statistics and figures", "has no idea what happens at the Old Market, how the city works" as he "leaves his desk only in October to take part in the marathon", and who is "only interested in mass events, whether sporting or business ones". His terms in office were seen as devastating for the city. However, the majority of the mayor's opponents were not against attracting big business to the city as such: they simply thought it was done in the wrong way. The mayor and his team's main fault was their detachment from the everyday life of urban dwellers and their inability to see that what really attracts capital to the city is the atmosphere of the place. The city could be indeed recognized as entrepreneurial if urban strategies of revitalization met local needs, as well as citizens' and visitors' expectations:

> Because the city is only interested in revenue, it raises rents for locals in the centre and builds new flats, and as a result we have an empty centre with just a few banks and pharmacies, and no people, no activity, no life in the city. It is not just a matter of taste or political views, but whether we want the city to develop, whether we want an attractive public space, or whether we just want to be a stop on a way from Warsaw to Berlin, associated with the shopping mall at the station. This is how Poznań thinks: first, the investors who built and lent expensive space, which is not affordable for most, and that leaves the centre empty, with empty premises.... But first we have to make sure this place is attractive, first we have to think of people, make their life more comfortable, enable them to cycle from one part of the city to another, protect green areas and create spaces, where you can enjoy your coffee. *This is what really attracts investors.*

David Harvey notices that the neoliberal system and capital accumulation depend on the popularity of middle-class values: "defenders of this regime of rights plausibly argue that it encourages 'bourgeois virtues', without which everyone in the world would be far worse off. These include individual responsibility and liability; independence from state interference...; equality of opportunity in the market and before the law; rewards for initiative and entrepreneurial endeavour; care for oneself and one's own; and an open marketplace that allows wide-ranging freedoms of choice in terms of both contract and exchange" (Harvey 2005: 181). But the local community took questions of individual freedom and initiative seriously and opposed it to government's authoritarianism and unfavourable elitist politics (cf. Harvey 2005: 175–6). Similarly as in Vancouver, where local community called upon individual freedom and middle-class values to fight unwanted investment in the area (Lowes 2002), the opposition juxtaposed the local middle-class ethos to with the "oligarchic" rules of union between politicians and big business.

However, as Harvey concludes, as long as those values remain unquestioned, we "accept that we have no alternative except to live under a regime of endless capital accumulation and economic growth no matter what the social, ecological, or political consequences" (Harvey 2005: 181–2). We remain "beggars [who] live off the crumbs from the rich man's table" (181). For him, the slogan "the city is not a company" could be a serious proposition as long as it "specif[ied] an alternative social process within which such alternative rights can inhere" (204). This would mean the systemic opposition should refrain from calling upon middle-class virtues. This reference worked so well, because it was embedded in the articulated tradition of a Prussian-like, bourgeois city of resourceful and thrifty citizens. A systemic change, therefore, would require rearticulating this tradition anew (Clifford 2001).

The discussion which followed in the wake of Euro 2012 led to the challenging of the dominant discourse, which had been hegemonic in the city for decades. Forces and visions struggling for power referred to the local ethos and values, and the election of a new mayor in autumn 2014 seemed to prove the victory of the former opposition, which had challenged the way the city had been governed. The case of the Youth Olympic Games, which the City Council did not agree to host, as well as the referendum on Cracow's bid for the 2022 Winter Olympics and the subsequent withdrawal of this bid after 70% of the citizens voted against it (Olimpijskie referendum 2014), illustrates a certain change in modernization processes in Poland. It also signalled the moment of crisis, when meanings and knowledge which used to work became the subject of negotiation.

In Poznań, the new mayor was elected as the strongest candidate against Ryszard Grobelny. Since 2014, his liberal views and decisions – although they gained him a lot of sympathy among certain citizens – are strongly criticized by more conservative circles. In their critique, they also refer to local bourgeois values, but call upon different characteristics – such as, for instance, Catholicism. Articulating the local tradition is an open-ended process, historically and politically constrained (Clifford 2001: 478). Interestingly, the former mayor fostered the Catholic traditions and remained in good relations with the Church. Catholicism as Poznanians' distinguishing characteristics was never, therefore, raised as an argument in the heated discussions about the local tradition and character which I heard and conducted during my research.

Old orders were indeed questioned, not only in Poznań, but across Poland in 2015 during the presidential and parliamentary elections. New ones are still under construction: new meanings of such term as modernization, democracy and politics, but also of national identity and "Poland" are being extensively negotiated. My field-site can only be seen as "a window into complexity, and never a holistic entity to be explained" (Candea 2007: 181), but I am arguing that recent political decisions of local and national politics triggered a debate about "collective imaginations", the legacy of the transition and the country's future. I used Euro 2012 as a lens that permits the casting of light onto currents which define the processes of imagining community (Anderson 1991) and constructing social space (Lefebvre 1991). I hope I have managed to present this space as a lively place, not as a fossil, and its people as shaping their identity towards and against the setting which they simultaneously actively produce.

Bibliography

M. Abélès (1988) 'Modern Political Ritual: Ethnography of an Inauguration and a Pilgrimage by President Mitterrand' In: *Current Anthropology* 23, 3, 391–404.

About the city (2012) *Poznań – The Host City of the UEFA EURO 2012*, http://www.poznan.pl/mim/uefaeuro2012/en/-,p,20892.html, date accessed 28.01.2016

T. Achrem (2007) Dziesięć mitów o Euro 2012 In: *Gazeta Wyborcza. Dodatek poznański*, nr 180, 03.08.2007

B. Anderson (1991) *Imagined Communities.* London: Verso

K. Anderson (2010) *Marx at the Margins. On Nationalism, Ethnicity, and Non-Western Societies.* Chicago: Chicago University Press

L. Arena and E. Molloy (2010) The Governance Paradox in Megaprojects. Entretiens Jacques Cartier, Lyon, France, https://halshs.archives-ouvertes.fr/halshs-00721622

W. Bartkowiak (2013) 'Panujący i poddani. Ranking prezydentów polskich miast 2013' In: *Gazeta Wyborcza*, nr 273. 8002, 23–24.11.2013

G. Baumann (2005) 'Grammars of Identity and Alterity' In: G. Bauman and A. Gnigrich (eds.) *Grammars of Identity and Alterity.* Oxford: Berghahn

© The Author(s) 2017

131

M.Z. Kowalska, *Urban Politics of a Sporting Mega Event*,
Football Research in an Enlarged Europe,
DOI 10.1007/978-3-319-52105-3

J. K. Bielecki (2014) 'Jak kusi kasa. Spowiedź liberała. Z Janem Krzysztofem Bieleckim rozmawia Grzegorz Sroczyński' In: *Gazeta Wyborcza*, no. 113. 8145, 7–8.5.2014, 14–16

M. Bloch (ed.) (1975) *Political Language, Oratory and Traditional Society.* London: Academic Press

D. Bohle and B. Greskovits (2007) 'Neoliberalism, Embedded Neoliberalism and Neocorporatism: Towards Transnational Capitalism in Central-Eastern Europe' In: *West European Politics* 30, 3, 443–66

L. Bojarski (2007) 'Życzenia na Euro 2012' In: *Gazeta Wyborcza. Dodatek Poznański* 246, 20.10.2007, 3

Z. Boniek (2012) 'To będzie udany turniej. Ze Zbigniewem Bońkiem rozmawia Przemysław Rudzki' In: *Fakt Sport*, nr 1/2012 Mistrzostwa Europy Polska-Ukraina 2012, 2

Brakuje 51 milionów (2012) *Brakuje 51 milionów. Te cięcia zabolą każdego z nas*, http://poznan.gazeta.pl/poznan/1,36037,12381445,Brakuje_51_milio now__Te_ciecia_zabola_kazdego_z_nas.html, date accessed 7.04.2014

N. Brenner (2011) 'The Urban Question and the Scale Question. Some Conceptual Clarifications' In N. Glick Schiller and A. Çağlar (ed.) *Locating Migration. Rescaling Cities and Migrants.* Ithaca and London: Cornell University Press, 23–41

N. Brenner and N. Theodore (2002a) 'Cities and Geographies of "Actually Existing Neoliberalism"' In *Antipode* 34, 3, 349–79

N. Brenner and N. Theodore (2002b) *Spaces of Neoliberalism: Urban Restructuring in North America and Western Europe.* Oxford: Blackwell

N. Brenner, B. Jessop, M. Jones, and G. MacLeod (2003) 'Introduction: State Space in Question' In: N. Brenner, B. Jessop, M. Jones, G. MacLeod (eds.) *State/Space: A Reader.* Oxford: Blackwell, 1–26

M. Buchowski (1997) *Reluctant Capitalists. Class and Culture in a Local Community in Western Poland.* Berlin: Centre Marc Bloch

M. Buchowski (2001) *Rethinking Transformation. An Anthropological Perspective on Post-socialism.* Poznań: Humaniora

M. Buchowski (2006) 'The Specter of Orientalism in Europe: From Exotic Other to Stigmatized Brother' In *Anthropological Quarterly* 79, 3, 463–82

M. Buchowski (2012) 'Europe as a Fortress: The End of Multiculturalism and The Rise of "Cultural Racism"' In: A. M. Kuznetsov (ed.) *Ethnic Politics and Non-military Aspects of Security.* Vladivostok: Far Eastern University, 33–46

M. Buchowski and J. Schmidt (2012) 'Imigracja a heterogeniczność kulturowa. Perspektywa antropologiczna' (Immigration and Cultural Heterogeneity: An Anthropological Perspective) In: M. Buchowski and J. Schmidt (eds.) *Migracje a heterogeniczność kulturowa. Na podstawie badań antropologicznych w Poznaniu (Migration and Cultural Heterogeneity: Anthropological Research in Poznań)*. Poznań: Nauka i Innowacje, 7–22

M. Buchowski (2015) 'Marx for Poles' In: *Dialectical Anthropology* 39, 2, 219–23

M. Buchowski and M. Kowalska (2015) 'Doing Ethnography and Writing Anthropology of an Event: The Protest Against the 2012 UEFA European Championship in Poznań' In B. Alpan, A. Schwell and A. Sonntag (eds.) *The European Football Championship. Mega-Event and Vanity Fair.* London: Palgrave Macmillan, 150–72

M. Buchowski, E. Conte, and C. Nagengast (eds.) (2001) *Poland Beyond Communism: "Transition" in Critical Perspective.* Fribourg: University Press

S. Bujalski, P. Wesołowski and E. Karendys (2012) 'Wiatr hula na stadionach. Ale nie w halach' In: *Gazeta Wyborcza* no. 296. 8025, 20.12.2012, 22–3

J. Butler (2001) *What Is Critique? An Essay on Foucault's Virtue*, http://eipcp.net/transversal/0806/butler/en, date accessed 28.01.2017

A. Çağlar (2010) 'Rescaling Cities, Cultural Diversity and Transnationalism: Migrants of Mardin and Essen' In: S. Vertovec (ed.) *Anthropology of Migration and Multiculturalism. New Directions.* London: Routledge, 113–38

M. Callon (ed.) (1998) *The Laws of the Market.* London: Blackwell

M. Callon (2007) 'What Does It Mean to Say That Economics Is Performative?' In: D. MacKenzie, F. Muniesa, and L. Siu (eds.) *Do Economists Make Market? On the Performativity of Economics.* Princeton and Oxford: Princeton University Press, 311–57

M. Candea (2007) 'Arbitrary Locations: In Defence of the Bounded Field-Site' In: *Journal of the Royal Anthropological Institute* (N.S.) 13, 167–84

M. Candea (2011) '"Our Division of the Universe". Making a Space for the Non-political in the Anthropology of Politics' In: *Current Anthropology* 52, 3, June 2011, 309–34

CBOS (2013) *Rok po Euro 2012. Komunikat z badań*, http://www.cbos.pl/SPISKOM.POL/2013/K_088_13.PDF, date accessed 28.01.2017

Chleba zamiast igrzysk (2012), https://chlebazamiastigrzysk.wordpress.com/, date accessed 28.01.2017

Cięcia w budżecie (2012) *Cięcia w budżecie. Oni źle rządzili, a my musimy płacić*, http://poznan.gazeta.pl/poznan/1,36037,12375209,Ciecia_w_budze

cie__Oni_zle_rzadzili__a_my_musimy_placic_.html,   date   accessed 7.04.2014

J. Clifford (2001) 'Indigenous Articulations' In: *The Contemporary Pacific* 13, 2, 468–90

J. Comaroff and J. Comaroff (1991) *Of Revelation and Revolution: Christianity, Colonialism and Consciousness in South Africa*. Chicago: Chicago University Press

J. Comaroff and J. Comaroff (1992) *Ethnography and the Historical Imagination*. Boulder, CO: Westview

J. Comaroff and J. Comaroff (2012) *Theory from the South: Or, How Euro-America Is Evolving Toward Africa*. Boulder and London: Paradigm Publishers

E. Conte and C. Giordano (1999) 'Pathways of Lost Rurality. Reflections on Post-socialism' In: Conte and Giordano (eds.) *Es war einam die Wende…Sozialer Umbruch der Landlichen Gesselscahten Mittel- und Sudeuropas*. Berlin: Centre Marc Bloch, 5–33

J. A. Davis (2012) *The Olympic Effect: How Sports Marketing Builds Strong Brands*. Singapore: John Wiley and Sons

G. Deleuze and F. Guattari (2009 [1972]) *Anti-Oedipus. Capitalism and Schizophrenia*. London: Penguin Classics

Deloitte (2012) *Raport: Podsumowanie kosztów i oszacowanie korzyści z organizacji turnieju UEFA EURO 2012*. Deloitte Polska

M. Douglas (1986) *How Institutions Think*. Syracuse: Syracuse University Press

J. Drahokoupil (2008) *Globalization and the State in Central and Eastern Europe. The Politics of Foreign Direct Investment*. London: Routledge

R. Drozdowski (2012) 'Nie wstydź się, że jesteś piknikiem. Z prof. Rafałem Drozdowskim rozmawia Piotr Bojarski' In: *Gazeta Wyborcza. Dodatek poznański* 12.06.2012, 10–11

E. C. Dunn (2004) *Privatizing Poland. Baby Food, Big Business, and the Remaking of Labor*. Ithaca: Cornell University Press

Z. Dworecki (1994) *Poznań i poznaniacy w Drugiej Rzeczypospolitej 1918–1939*. Poznań: Wydawnictwo Media Rodzina

Euro to boost economy (2012) *Poland Will Use Euro 2012 to Boost Economy and Global Image, Says Sports Minister*, http://www.insideworldfootball.com/world-tournaments/european-championship/10286-poland-will-use-euro-2012-to-boost-economy-and-global-image-says-sports-minister, date accessed 28.01.2017

Euro to sukces organizacyjny (2012) *Prezydent Poznania: Euro to sukces orga-nizacyjny, nie finansowy*, http://www.gloswielkopolski.pl/artykul/633675,rys zard-grobelny-euro-to-sukces-organizacyjny-a-nie-finansowy,id,t.html, date accessed 28.01.2017

N. Fairclough (2001) [1989] *Language and Power*. London: Longman

J. Ferguson (2010) 'The Uses of Neoliberalism' In: *Antipode* 41, Supplement s1, 166–84

J. Ferguson (2014) *Give a Man a Fish. Reflections of the New Politics of Distribution*. Durham and London: Duke University Press

Fitch potwierdził ratingi (2014) 'Fitch potwierdził ratingi A- Poznania z perspektywą stabilną' In: *Gazeta Wyborcza*, http://wyborcza.biz/Gieldy/ 1,132329,15868864,Fitch_potwierdzil_ratingi_A__Poznania_z_perspek tywa.html, date accessed 14.03.2015

L. Fleck (1979 [1935]) *Genesis and Development of Scientific Fact [Entstehung und Entwicklung einer wissenschaftlichen Tatsache*, translated in 1979 by F. Bradley and T. J. Trenn]. Chicago and London: The University of Chicago Press

B. Flyvbjerg (2013) 'Mega Delusional: The Curse of Megaproject", In: *New Scientist*, December, 28–9, http://bit.ly/19QErEn, date accessed 28.01.2017

B. Flyvbjerg (2014) 'What You Should Know About Megaprojects and Why: An Overview' In: *Project Management Journal* 45, 2, 6–19

B. Flyvbjerg (2017) 'Megaprojects: Over Budget, Over Time, Over and Over' In: *Cato Policy Report*, 39, 1, 5–8

B. Flyvbjerg, N. Bruzelius, and W. Rothengatter (2003) *Megaprojects and Risk. An Anatomy of Ambition*. Cambridge: Cambridge University Press

B. Flyvbjerg, T. Landman, and S. Schram (2013) 'Tension Points in Real Social Science: A Response' In: *The British Journal of Sociology* 64, 4, December, 758–62

E. Follath and J. Puhl (2012) 'Polska Jest Prima' In: *Forum* 22, 23, 28.05–10.06.2012, 4–9

M. Foucault (1997) *Ethics: Subjectivity and Truth. Essential Works of Michel Foucault, 1954–1984*. Vol 1, New York: New Press

W. Gadomski (2013) 'Od katastrofy do wolnego rynku. Jak Polska uciekła komornikowi spod młotka' In: *Gazeta Wyborcza*, no. 257. 7986, 4.11.2013, 20–1

C. Geertz (1995) *After the Fact: Two Countries, Four Decades, One Anthropologist*. Cambridge, Mass: Harvard University Press

C. Giordano (2009) 'Afterword – Under the Aegis of Anthropology: Blazing New Trails' In: L. Kürti and P. Skalník (eds.) *Postsocialist Europe: Anthropological Perspectives from Home.* New York and Oxford: Berghahn Books, 295–304.

N. Glick Schiller and A. Çağlar (2011a) 'Downscaled Cities and Migrant Pathways. Locality and Agency Without an Ethnic Lens' In: N. Glick Schiller and A. Çağlar (eds.) *Locating Migration. Rescaling Cities and Migrants.* Ithaca and London: Cornell University Press, 190–212

N. Glick Schiller and A. Çağlar (2011b) 'Introduction: Migrants and Cities' In: N. Glick Schiller and A. Çağlar (ed.) *Locating Migration. Rescaling Cities and Migrants.* Ithaca and London: Cornell University Press, 1–19

N. Glick Schiller and A. Çağlar (2011c) 'Locality and Globality. Building a Comparative Analytical Framework in Migration and Urban Studies' In: N. Glick Schiller and A. Çağlar (eds.) *Locating Migration. Rescaling Cities and Migrants.* Ithaca and London: Cornell University Press, 60–81

C. Gratton and I. Henry (eds.) (2001) *Sport in the City.* London: Routledge

C. Gregory (2009) 'Whatever Happened to Economic Anthropology?' In: *The Australian Journal of Anthropology* (2009) 20, 285–300

R. Grobelny (2012) 'Idee, które napędzają miasto' In: *Gazeta Wyborcza. Dodatek poznański* 23–24.06.2012, 10

R. Grobelny (2014) 'Będą o mnie pisać jak o Cyrylu Ratajskim. Z Ryszardem Grobelnym rozmawiają Piotr Bojarski, Seweryn Lipoński' In: *Gazeta Wyborcza. Dodatek Poznański* 05.12.2014, http://poznan.gazeta.pl/poznan/1,36037,17079516,Grobelny__Beda_o_mnie_pisac_jak_o_Cyrylu_Ratajskim.html#ixzz3RAlaDgRy, date accessed 28.01.2017

Grobelny buduje piramidy (2012) 'Grobelny buduje piramidy. Potem mamy egipskie ciemności' In: *Gazeta Wyborcza* 04.09.2012

Grobelny chce milionów (2012) *Grobelny chce milionów. Na igrzyska*, http://poznan.gazeta.pl/poznan/1,36001,12502914,Grobelny_chce_milionow__Na_igrzyska.html, date accessed 28.01.2017

R. Gruneau (2002) 'Foreword' In: M. D. Lowes (ed.) *Indy Dreams and Urban Nightmares. Speed Merchants, Spectacle, and the Struggle over Public Space in the World-Class City.* Toronto, Buffalo and London: University of Toronto Press, ix–xii

R. Gruneau and D. Whitson (1993) *Hockey Night in Canada: Sport, Identities, and Cultural Practices.* Toronto: Garamond

R. Grupiński (2014) *To jego ostatnia kadencja*, http://grupinski.pl/pl-news-full-1417.html, date accessed 28.01.2017

J. Guyer (2007) 'Prophecy and the Near Future: Thoughts of Macroeconomic, Evangelical, and Punctuated Time' In: *American Ethnologist* 34, 3, 409–21

C. M. Hall (2006) 'Urban Entrepreneurship, Corporate Interests and Sports Mega-Events: The Thin Policies of Competitiveness Within the Hard Outcomes of Neoliberalism' In: J. Horne and W. Manzenreiter (eds.) *The Sociological Review. Special Issue: Sociological Review Monograph Series: Sports Mega-Events: Social Scientific Analyses of a Global Phenomenon* 54, Supplement s2, 59–70

T. Hall and P. Hubbard (eds.) (1998) *The Entrepreneurial City: Geographies of Politics, Regime and Representation.* Chichester: John Wiley

C. Hann (1980) *Tazlar: A Village in Hungary.* Cambridge: Cambridge University Press.

A. Hanson (1989) 'The Making of the Maori: Culture Invention and Its Logic' In: *American Anthropologist, New Series* 91, 4, 890–902

C. Hann (ed.) (2002) *Postsocialism: Ideals, Ideologies and Practices in Eurasia.* London: Routledge.

C. Hann, M. Sárkány, and P. Skalnik (eds.) 2005. *Studying Peoples in the People's Democracies. Socialist Era Anthropology in East-Central Europe.* Münster: LIT Verlag

D. Harvey (1989a) *The Condition of Postmodernity.* Oxford: Blackwell

D. Harvey (1989b) 'From Managerialism to Entrepreneurialism: The Transformation in Urban Governance in Late Capitalism' In: *Geografiska Annaler. Series B, Human Geography, The Roots of Geographical Change: 1973 to the Present*, 71, 1, 3–17.

D. Harvey (2005) *A Brief History of Neoliberalism.* Oxford: Oxford University Press

M. Herzfeld (1992) *The Social Production of Indifference. Exploring the Symbolic Roots of Western Bureaucracy.* Chicago and London: University of Chicago Press

M. Herzfeld (2000) 'Uncanny Success. Some Closing Remarks' In: J. Pina-Cabral and A. Pedroso de Lima (eds.) *Elites Choice, Leadership and Succession.* Oxford and New York: Berg, 227–236

F. L. Hess (1996) 'Culture as Studied and Cultural Studies: An Interview with George Marcus' In: *Iowa Journal of Cultural Studies*, 67–80, http://ir.uiowa.edu/ijcs/vol1996/iss15/13, date accessed 28.01.2017

A. O. Hirschman (1995) *Development Projects Observed.* Washington, DC: Brookings Institution

K. Ho (2009) *Liquidated: An Ethnography of Wall Street.* New York City: Duke University Press

D. R. Holmes (2014) *Economy of Words. Communicative Imperatives in Central Banks.* Chicago and London: The University of Chicago Press

D. R. Holmes and G. Marcus (2005) 'Cultures of Expertise and the Management of Globalization: Toward the Re-functioning of Ethnography' In: A. Ong, S. J. Collier (eds.) *Global Assemblages. Technology, Politics, and Ethnics as Anthropological Problems.* Malden, Oxford and Carlton: Blackwell Publishing, 235–52

J. Horne and W. Menzenreiter (2006) 'An Introduction to the Sociology of Sports Mega-Events' In: J. Horne and W. Manzenreiter (eds.) *The Sociological Review. Special Issue: Sociological Review Monograph Series: Sports Mega-Events: Social Scientific Analyses of a Global Phenomenon* 54, Supplement s2, 1–24

C. Humphrey (1983) *Karl Marx Collective: Economy, Society and Religion in a Siberian Collective Farm.* Cambridge: Cambridge University Press.

B. R. Humphreys and S. Prokopowicz (2007) 'Assessing the Impact of Sports Mega-Events in Transition Economies: EURO 2012 in Poland and Ukraine' In: *Journal of Sport Management and Marketing* 2, 5/6, 496–509

Impact (2010) *Report on the Impact of Preparations For and Organization of UEFA Euro 2012 on Polish Economy Commissioned by a Special Purpose Vehicle of the Minister of Sport and Tourism.* PL.2012.Sp. z o.o., Warsaw

A. Jackson (ed.) (1987) *Anthropology at Home* London: Tavistock

Jak przyznali nam Euro (2012) 'Jak przyznali nam Euro' In: *Fakt Sport,* nr 1/ 2012 Mistrzostwa Europy Polska-Ukraina 2012, 10–11

M. Jamroż (2012) 'Nie jesteśmy prowincją (Co nam zostało po Euro)' In: *Gazeta Wyborcza* 27.06.2012, 5

K. Jasiecki (2013) *Kapitalizm po polsku. Między modernizacją a peryferiami Unii Europejskiej.* Warszawa: Wydawnictwo IFiS PAN

L. Jażdżewski (2015) 'Władza trwa. Na razie nic więcej. Czy ktoś trafi do młodych Polaków?' In: *Gazeta Wyborcza* no. 2. 8335, 3–4.1.2015, 18

B. Jessop (2013) [1997] 'The Entrepreneurial City: Re-imaging Localities, Redesigning Economic Governance, or Restructuring Capital?' in N. Jewson and S. MacGregor (eds.) *Realising Cities: New Spatial Divisions and Social Transformation.* London: Routledge, 28–41, http://bobjessop. org/2013/12/02/the-entrepreneurial-city-re-imaging-localities-re-designing-economic-governance-or-re-structuring-capital/, date accessed 28.01.2017

B. Jessop (2013) [1998] 'The Enterprise of Narrative and the Narrative of Enterprise: Place Marketing and the Entrepreneurial City' In: T. Hall and P. Hubbard eds. *The Entrepreneurial City*. Chichester: Wiley, 77–99, http://bobjessop.org/2013/12/03/the-narrative-of-enterprise-and-the-enterprise-of-narrative-place-marketing-and-the-entrepreneurial-city/, date accessed 28.01.2017

I. Kado and J. Kado (1967) 'Uprzemysłowienie Poznania a uprzemysłowienie Wielkopolski oraz skutki osadnicze tego procesu' In: J. Ziółkowski (1967) *Poznań. Społeczno-przestrzenne skutki industrializacji*. Warszawa: Państwowe Wydawnictwo Naukowe, 17–58

S. Karwowski (2005 [1907]) 'Kultura wielkopolska' In: W. Molik (ed.) *Etos Wielkopolan. Antologia tekstów o społeczeństwie Wielkopolski z drugiej połowy XIX i XX wieku*. Poznań: Wydawnictwo Poznańskiego Towarzystwa Przyjaciół Nauk, 85–9

L. Kiel (2014) 'Polska jako skolonizowany kolonizator. Dyskursy o "europejskości" w związku z Euro 2012' In: M. Buchowski and M. Kowalska (eds.) *Nie tylko piłka w grze*. Poznań: Wydawnictwo Nauka i Innowacje, 81–107

Kierownik budowy kłamał (2014) 'Kierownik budowy kłamał w sprawie izolacji' In: *Głos Wielkopolski* 26.03.2014, http://stadiony.net/aktualnosci/2014/03/poznan_kierownik_budowy_klamal_w_sprawie_izolacji

L. King (2007) 'Central European Capitalism in Comparative Perspective' In: B. Hancké, M. Rhodes, and M. Thatcher (eds.) *Beyond Varieties of Capitalism. Conflict, Contradictions, and Complementarities in the European Economy*. Oxford: Oxford University Press, 308–27

L. King and I. Szelenyi (2005) 'Post-communist Economic Systems' In: N.J. Smelser and R. Swedberg (eds.) *The Handbook of Economic Sociology*. Princeton: Princeton University Press, 205–32

B. Kisiel (2009) 'W 2010 miasto postawiło na inwestycje i...długi' In: *Głos Wielkopolski* 23.12.2009

V. Klemperer (2006) [1947] *The Language of the Third Reich*. London: Continuum

M. Kobosko (2012) 'Biją mnie Niemcy' In: *Wprost*, nr 23, 4–10.10.2012, 4

M. Kokot and M. Karbowiak (2012) 'Pusto wszędzie, biednie wszędzie' In: *Gazeta Wyborcza* 3–4.11.2012, 14–15

B. Komorowski (2013) 'Skrajności uwodzą, ale szybko rozczarowują. Z prezydentem Bronisławem Komorowskim rozmawiają Jarosław Kurski i Bartosz T. Wieliński' In: *Gazeta Wyborcza*, no. 126. 7855, 1–2.06.2013, 20–1

A. Kosek (2007) 'Nowoczesne city kosztem regionu' In: *Głos Wielkopolski* 10.12.2007

M. Kowalska (2014) 'The Mega-Event Paradox' In: *Sport and Citizenship. Sport Serving Society*, no. 29, December 2014, January–February 2015, 13

M. Kowalska (2016) 'Hegemony in Question? Euro 2012 and Local Politics in the City of Poznań' In: M. Buchowski, M. Kowalska, A. Schwell and N. Szogs (eds.) *New Ethnographies of Football in Europe: People, Passions, Politics*. Basingstoke: Palgrave.

M. Kowalska (2017) 'From Football Field to Communicative Field. Embedding Entrepreneurial Strategy and Negotiating Local Past and Future During Euro 2012 in the Host City of Poznań' In: *Anthropological Notebooks* 2017/1

M. W. Kozak (2015) 'Co wymyślili chodnik. Za unijne pieniądze przestajemy doganiać Zachód. Z Markiem W. Kozakiem rozmawia Grzegorz Sroczyński' In: *Gazeta Wyborcza. Magazyn Świąteczny*, no. 125. 8458, 30–31.05.2015, 14–16

M. Król (2014) 'Byliśmy głupi. Marcin Król w rozmowie z Grzegorzem' In: *Gazeta Wyborcza. Magazyn Świąteczny*, no. 32. 8064, 8–9.02. 2014, 12–14

W. Kruk (2013) 'Świetności Św. Marcina nie da się przywrócić' In: *Gazeta Wyborcza. Dodatek Poznański* 10.02.2013, http://poznan.gazeta.pl/poznan/ 1,36037,13373202,Wojciech_Kruk__Swietnosci_Sw__Marcina_nie_da_ sie_przywrocic.html, date accessed 28.01.2017

P. Kuczyński (2013) 'Ile kosztuje zwariowany świat? Z Piotrem Kuczyńskim rozmawia Grzegorz Sroczyński' In: *Gazeta Wyborcza. Magazyn Świąteczny*, no. 156. 7885, 6–7.07.2013, 20–2

D. Lane and M. Myant (2007) *Varietes of Capitalism in Post-communist Countries* New York: Palgrave Macmillan

E. Leach (1982) *Social Anthropology*. Oxford: Oxford University Press

H. Lefebvre (1991) *The Production of Space*. Oxford, UK and Cambridge, USA: Wiley-Blackwell

A. Leszczyński (2014) 'Nie zarabiasz? Zdechnij' In: *Gazeta Wyborcza*, no. 68. 8100, 22–23.03.2014

S. Lipoński (2013a) 'Sondaż "Gazety" na rok przed wyborami samorządowymi. Wyzwania dla Poznania' In: *Gazeta Wyborcza, Dodatek poznański* 23–24.11.2013

S. Lipoński (2013b) 'Jaki faraon, taka piramida. Po ostrej dyskusji Poznań ma budżet na 2014 rok' In: *Gazeta Wyborcza. Dodatek Poznański* 20.12.2013

S. Lipoński (2013c) 'Budżet 2014 Poznań już ma, ale nie za darmo' In: *Gazeta Wyborcza. Dodatek poznański* 21–22.12.2013, 1

D. Lipton and J. Sachs (1990) 'Creating a Market Economy in Eastern Europe: The Case of Poland' In: *Brooking Papers on Economic Activity* 1990, 1, 75–147

A. Lise and E. Molloy (2012) 'The Governance Paradox in Megaprojects' In: *Communication et grands projets: Les nouveaux défis.* (provisional title) [Author manuscript, published in France: Entretiens Jacques Cartier, Lyon (2010)]

M. D. Lowes (2002) *Indy Dreams and Urban Nightmares. Speed Merchants, Spectacle, and the Struggle over Public Space in the World-Class City.* Toronto, Buffalo and London: University of Toronto Press Incorporated

W. Lubański (2012) 'Najważniejsze wydarzenie' In: *Wprost,* nr 23, 4–10.10.2012, 53

D. MacKenzie (2006) 'Is Economics Performative? Option Theory and the Construction of Derivative Markets' In: *Journal of the History of Economic Thought* 28, 1, 29–55

M. Malfas, E. Theodoraki, and B. Houlihan (2004) 'Impacts of the Olympic Games as Mega-Events' In: *Municipal Engineer* 157, ME3, 209–20

G. E. Marcus (1998) *Ethnography Through Thick and Thin.* Princeton: Princeton University Press

G. E. Marcus and M. Fischer (1999) [1986] *Anthropology as Cultural Critique. An Experimental Moment in the Human Sciences.* Chicago: University of Chicago Press

Z. Marecki (2011) 'Piękne stadiony z niepewną przyszłością' In: *Raport Wspólnoty* Wspólnota 35, 8, 35, 27.08.2011, http://www.wspolnota.org.pl/index.php?id=9&tx_news_pi1[controller]=News&tx_news_pi1[action]=detail&tx_news_pi1[news]=24624&cHash=acb3a5a11c446e5a933752450cf25c56, date accessed 28.01.2017

J. Mazurczak (2012) 'Irlandczycy już wracają. Rozmowa o Euro 2012 z Janem Mazurczakiem, szefem Poznańskiej Lokalnej Organizacji Turystycznej' In: *Gazeta Wyborcza. Dodatek poznański,* nr 157. 7581, 7–9.07.2012, 2

A. Mencwel (2014) 'Kiedy Polska będzie nowoczesna. Z prof. Andrzejem Mencwelem rozmawia Jarosław Mikołajewski' In: *Gazeta Wyborcza. Magazyn Świąteczny,* no. 131. 8163, 7–8.06.2014, 12–14

L. Mergler and K. Pobłocki (2010) 'Nic o nas bez nas: polityka skali a demokracja miejska' In: *Res Publica Nowa* 11–12 (201–2), 7–14

Miasto może odzyskać pieniądze za remont (2014) Miasto może odzyskać pieniądze za remont INEA stadionu PAP 6.11.2014, http://stadiony.net/aktualnosci/2014/11/poznan_miasto_moze_odzyskac_pieniadze_za_remont_inea_stadionu, date accessed 28.01.2017

Ministry of Sports and Tourism (2012) The Polish Effect: The Success of Euro 2012 Beyond Expectations, http://en.msport.gov.pl/article/the-polish-effect-the-success-of-euro-2012-beyond-expectations, date accessed 28.01.2017

Minutes 36 (2012) *Protokół nr 36/2012 XXXVI sesji Rady Miasta Poznania z dnia 4 września 2012 roku* (bip.poznan.pl)

Minutes 61 (2013) *Protokół Nr LXI/2013 LXI sesji budżetowej Rady Miasta Poznania z dnia 20 grudnia 2013 r.* (bip.poznan.pl)

MIO 2018 nie (2012) Młodzieżowe Igrzyska Olimpijskie 2018 nie w Poznaniu, http://www.wprost.pl/ar/351660/Mlodziezowe-igrzyska-olimpijskie-2018-nie-w-Poznaniu/PUB, date accessed 01.07.2015

K. Modzelewski (2013) 'Wkurzył się Pan? Świetnie! Z Karolem Modzelewskim rozmawia Grzegorz Sroczyński' In: *Gazeta Wyborcza*, no. 215. 7944, 14–15.09.2013, 14–17

E. Mokrzycki (2001) *Bilans niesentymentalny*. Warszawa: Wydawnictwo IFiS PAN

Monitor Wielkopolski (2008) 'Monitor Wielkopolski' In: *Głos Wielkopolski* 13.08.2008

J. Mucha (2012) 'Strategia na medale. Radosław Leniarski rozmawia z Ministrą Sportu i Turystyki Joanną Muchą' In: *Gazeta Wyborcza*, no. 193. 7617, 20.08.2012, 5

L. Nader (1972) [1969] 'Up the Anthropologist – Perspectives Gained from Studying Up' In: D. Hymes (ed.) *Reinventing Anthropology*. New York: Pantheon Books, 284–311

C. Nagengast (1991) *Reluctant Socialists, Rural Entrepreneurs. Class, Culture, and the Polish State*. Boulder, San Francisco and Oxford: Westview Press

L. B. Namier (2013) [1946] *1848 – Rewolucja intelektualistów*. Wydawnictwo Universitas: Kraków

S. Narotzky and N. Besnier (2014) 'Crisis, Value, and Hoper: Rethinking the Economy. An Introduction to Supplement 9' In: *Current Anthropology* 55, 9, August 2014, S4–S16

R. Nawrot (2008) 'Słono zapłacą za Euro' In: *Gazeta Wyborcza. Dodatek Poznański* 07.02.2008

A. Nölke and A. Vliegenthart (2009) 'Enlarging the Varietes of Capitalism: The Emergence of Dependent Market Economies in East Central Europe' In: *World Politics* 4, 670–702

Ocena ratingowa Poznania (2014), http://bip.poznan.pl/bip/ocena-ratingowa-poznania,doc,291/ocena-ratingowa-poznania,1742.html, date accessed 28.01.2017

Olimpijskie referendum (2014) *Olimpijskie referendum razem z eurowyborami. Kraków zagłosuje 25 maja*, http://wyborcza.pl/1,75478,15725695,Olimpijskie_referendum_razem_z_eurowyborami__Krakow.html, date accessed 28.01.2017

L. Oręziak (2013) 'Myślisz, że sam sobie poradzisz? Prof. Leokadia Oręziak w rozmowie z Grzegorzem Sroczyńskim' In: *Gazeta Wyborcza. Magazyn Świąteczny*, 3–4.08.2013, http://wyborcza.pl/magazyn/1,133673,14380111, Myslisz__ze_sam_sobie_poradzisz_.html, date accessed 28.01.2017

M. Orenstein (2014) 'Jak wysoko poleci Polska?' In: *Gazeta Wyborcza*, nr 8. 8040, 11–12.01.2014

D. Ost (2005) *Deafeat of Solidarity. Anger and Politics in Postcommunist Europe*. Ithaca: Cornell University Press

D. Ost (2014) 'Nie byliście głupi. Budujcie Polskę Waszych marzeń. Z prof. Davidem Ostem rozmawia Adam Leszczyński' In: *Gazeta Wyborcza*, no. 148. 8180, 28–29.06.2014, 32

M. Osterweil (2014) 'Social Movements' In: Donald M. Nonini (ed.) *A Companion to Urban Anthropology*. Chichester and Malden: Wiley-Blackwell

A. Ouroussoff (2010) *Wall Street at War: The Secret Struggle for the Global Economy*. Cambridge and Malden: Polity Press

C. Palmer (1998) 'Le Tour du Monde: Towards an Anthropology of the Global Mega-Event' In: *The Australian Journal of Anthropology* 9, 3, 265–73

PeWuKa Bis (2014) 'PeWuKa Bis. Dodatek na 25-lecie wolnej Polski' In: *Gazeta Wyborcza, Dodatek poznański* 125. 8157, 31.05.2014

K. Pobłocki (2012) 'Taniec z gwiazdami, czyli Jan Gehl w objęciach Ryszarda Grobelnego' In: *Res Publica nova* 31.08.2012

K. Polanyi (2001 [1944]) *The Great Transformation: The Political and Economic Origins of Our Time*. Boston: Beacon Press

Ponad 20 mln debetu (2012) *Prezydent Poznania: Ponad 20 mln debetu na Euro 2012*, http://wyborcza.biz/biznes/10,100970,12202051,prezydent-poznania-ponad-20-milionow-zlotych-debetu-na-euro.html?disableRedirects=true#ixzz21q0WB66P, date accessed 28.01.2017

Prezydent chciałby podnieść czynsz Lechowi (2015), http://stadiony.net/aktualnosci/2015/02/poznan_prezydent_chcialby_podniesc_czynsz_lechowi, date accessed 28.01.2017

A. Przybylska (2008) 'Rząd da Poznaniowi mniej niż jedną trzecią na budowę stadionu' In: *Gazeta Wyborcza. Dodatek Poznański* 05.02.2008

PWC (2007) *Raport na temat wielkich polskich miast. Poznań* (Raport z 2006), http://www.pwc.pl/pl/sektor-publiczny/raporty_poznan-pol.pdf, date accessed 28.01.2017

PWC (2011) *Reports on Major Polish Cities. Poznań* (Raport z 2010), http://www.pwc.pl/en/wielkie-miasta-polski/raport_Poznan_eng.pdf, date accessed 01.07.2015

P. Rabinow (ed.) (1991) *The Foucault Reader: An Introduction to Foucault's Thought.* London: Penguin

Raport Euro 2012 no 1 (2012) *Podsumowanie wizerunkowe UEFA Euro. Podsumowanie wizerunkowe.* Materiały Miasta Gospodarza

Raport Euro 2012 no 2 (2012) *Ekonomiczne efekty bezpośrednio związane z turniejem UEFA Euro.* Materiały Miasta Gospodarza

Raport o stanie miasta (2013) *Poznań. Raport o stanie miasta* Wydział Rozwoju Miasta Urzędu Miasta Poznania, www.poznan.pl/fakty_liczby

A. Rembowski (2007) 'Euro 2012 zmieni Poznań w miasto marzeń' In: *Gazeta Wyborcza. Dodatek Poznański* 20.11.2007

M. Roche (2000) *Mega-Events and Modernity.* London: Routledge

N. Rose (1999) *Powers of Freedom. Reframing Political Thought.* Cambridge: Cambridge University Press

N. Rose, P. O'Malley, and M. Valverde (2006) 'Governmentality' In: *Annual Review of Law and Social Science* 2, 83–104

J. Rutkowski (2013) 'Polskie buraki kontra niemieckie procesory. Dlaczego w porównaniu z Francuzami i Niemcami zarabiamy tak strasznie mało?' In: *Gazeta Wyborcza*, no. 210. 7939, 9.09.2013, 16–17

C. F. Sabel (1989) 'Flexible Specialization and the Re-emergence of Regional Economies' In: P. Hirst and J. Zeitlin (eds) *Reversing Industrial Decline? Industrial Structure and Policy in Britain and Her Competitors.* Oxford: Berg, 17–70

M. Sahlins M (1983) 'Other Times, Other Customs: The Anthropology of History' In: *American Anthropologist, New Series* 85, 3, 517–44

M. Sahlins (1985) *Islands of History.* Chicago: The University of Chicago Press

S. Sassen (1994) *Cities in the World Economy.* London: New Pine Press

S. Sassen (1996) 'Whose City Is It? Globalization and the Formation of New Claims', In: *Public Culture* 8, 205–23

J. Sawka (2012) 'My we Wrocławiu i tak swoje wygraliśmy' In: *Gazeta Wyborcza* 26.06.2012

A. Sayer and R. Walker (1992) *The New Social Economy: Reworking the Division of Labor.* Cambridge, MA: Blackwell

W. Schiffauer (1997) *Fremde in der Stadt.* Frankfurt/Main: Suhrkamp

K. Schimmel (1995) 'Growth Politics, Urban Development, and Sports Stadium Construction in the United States: A Case Study' In: J. Bale and O. Moen (eds.) *The Stadium and the City.* Keele, Staffordshire: Keele University Press, 115–56

D. C. Schneider (2012) *Being Góral: An Identity Politics and Globalization in Postsocialist Poland.* Albany: SUNY Press

C. Shore (2000) *Building Europe. The Cultural Politics of European Integration.* London and New York: Routledge

C. Shore (2002) 'Introduction: Towards an Anthropology of Elites' In: C. Shore and S. Nugent (eds.) *Elite Cultures. Anthropological Perspectives.* London and New York: Routledge, 1–21

C. Shore (2014) 'Anthropology and Political Leadership' In: *Oxford Handbook of Political Leadership.* Oxford: Oxford University Press, 176–92

C. Shore and S. Wright (eds.) (1997) *Anthropology of Policy. Critical Perspectives on Governance and Power.* London and New York: Routledge

C. Shore and S. Wright (2011) 'Conceptualising Policy: Technologies of Governance and the Politics of Visibility' In: C. Shore, S. Wright and D. Però (eds.) *Policy Worlds. Anthropology and the Analysis of Contemporary Power.* Oxford, New York: Berghahn Books, 1–25

S. Sierakowski (2014) 'Tęsknię za facetami w swetrach. Jak zorganizować społeczeństwo, żeby nam się lepiej żyło? Ze Sławomirem Sierakowskim rozmawia Grzegorz Sroczyński' In: *Gazeta Wyborcza,* no. 93. 7823, 20–21.04.2013, 26–7

G. Smith (1999) *Confronting the Present. Towards a Politically Engaged Anthropology.* Oxford and New York: Berg

N. Smith (2003) 'Remaking Scale: Competition and Cooperation in Pre-national and Post-national Europe' In: N. Brenner, B. Jessop, M. Jones, G. MacLeod (eds.) *State/Space: A Reader.* Oxford: Blackwell, 225–38

J. Stacul (2014) 'The Production of "Local Culture" in Post-socialist Poland' In: *Anthropological Journal of European Cultures* 23, 1, 21–39

Stadion Lecha (2012), http://stadiumdb.com/stadiums/pol/stadion_lecha_poz nan, date accessed 28.01.2017

Stadion miejski w Poznaniu (2012) Prezentacja. Komisja Kultury Fizycznej, Sportu i Turystyki w Warszawie, 13 września 2012 (materiały organizatora)

Stadiony (2012) www.stadiony.net/projekty/pol, date accessed 28.01.2017

Strategy (2013) *Strategia Rozwoju Miasta Poznania do roku 2030. Aktualizacja 2013,* http://www.poznan.pl/mim/main/strategia-rozwoju-miasta-poznania-do-roku-2030-aktualizacja-2013,p,14886,26640,26644.html, date accessed 28.01.2017

T. Stryjakiewicz, T. Kaczmarek, M. Meczynski, J. J. Parysek, and K. Stachowiak (2007) *Poznan Faces the Future. Pathways to Creative and Knowledge-Based Regions. ACRE Report WP2.8.* Amsterdam: AMIDSt, http://acre.socsci.uva.nl/results/documents/WP2.8Poznan_FINAL.pdf, date accessed 28.01.2017

T. Stryjakiewicz, T. Kaczmarek, M. Meczynski, J. J. Parysek, and K. Stachowiak (2010) *Policies and Strategies in Poznan. How to Enhance the City's Competitiveness. ACRE Report WP10.8.* Amsterdam: AISSR, http://acre.socsci.uva.nl/results/documents/wp10.8poznan-FINAL.pdf, date accessed 28.01.2017

J. Suchecka (2012) 'Wielka organizatorka. Kobieta od Strefy Kibica: Katarzyna Parysek' In: *Gazeta Wyborcza. Dodatek poznański* 2–3.06.2012, 12

E. Swyngedouw (1997) 'Neither Global nor Local: "Glocalization" and the Politics of Scale', In: K. Fox (ed.) *Spaces of Globalization: Reasserting the Power of the Local.* New York: Guilford, 137–66

E. Swyngedouw, F. Moulaert, and A. Rodriguez (2002) 'Neoliberal Urbanization in Europe: Large-Scale Urban Development Projects and the New Urban Policy' In: *Antipode* 34, 3, 542–77

M. Thatcher (1981) 'Mrs. Thatcher: The First Two Years. Economics are the Method: The Object Is to Change the Soul. Interviewed by Ronald Butt' In: *Sunday Times* 3.05.1981, http://www.margaretthatcher.org/document/104475, date accessed 28.01.2017

A. Thomas (2014) 'Berlin Mayor to Resign After Criticism' In: *The Wall Street Journal* 26.08.2014, http://www.wsj.com/articles/berlin-mayor-resigns-after-criticism-over-delays-to-new-airport-opening-1409056774, date accessed 28.01.2017

E. Thompson (1968) *The Making of the English Working Class: The Origin of the Black Act.* Harmondsworth: Penguin

D. Tusk (2007) '20 pytań do...Donalda Tuska. W rozmowie z Erykiem Stankunowiczem' In: *Forbes* 01.09.2007

D. Tusk (2013a) 'Nie jestem liderem salonowej rewolucji. Premier Donald Tusk w rozmowie z Dominiką Wielowieyską' In: *Gazeta Wyborcza*, no. 64. 7794, 16–17.03.2013, 14–16

D. Tusk (2013b) 'Jestem liderem, nie kilerem. Z premierem Donaldem Tuskiem rozmawiają Jarosław Kurski i Adam Michnik' In: *Gazeta Wyborcza*, no. 156. 7885, 6–7.07.2013, 12–14

UEFA (2013) *UEFA Financial Report 2011/2012.* XXXVII Ordinary UEFA Congress London, 24.05.2013, http://www.uefa.org/MultimediaFiles/Download/EuroExperience/uefaorg/Finance/01/95/54/65/1955465_DOWNLOAD.pdf, date accessed 28.01.2017

K. Verdery (1996) *What Was Socialism, and What Comes Next?* Princeton: Princeton University Press

M. Verlot (2001) 'Are Politicians Human? Problems and Challenges of Institutional Anthropology' In: *Social Anthropology* 9, 3, 345–53

B. Vidacs (2010) *Visions of a Better World. Football in the Cameroonian Social Imagination.* Münster: Lit Verlag

A. Walicki (2013a) 'Reforma nauki w Polsce, czyli/Nieświęty sojusz biurokracji z rynkiem' In: *Gazeta Wyborcza*, no. 126. 7855, 1–2.06.2013, 22–3

A. Walicki (2013b) 'Neoliberalna kontrrewolucja. Stworzyliśmy świat gigantycznych możliwości' In: *Gazeta Wyborcza*, no. 279. 8008, 30.11–1.12.2013, 30–1

J. Wedel (1992) *The Unplanned Society: Poland During and After Communism.* New York: Columbia University Press

J. Wedel (2001) *Collision and Collusion: The Strange Case of Western Aid to Eastern Europe.* New York: Palgrave

J. Wedel (2011) [2009] *Shadow Elite: How the World's New Power Brokers Undermine Democracy, Government, and the Free Market.* New York: Basic Books

J. R. Wedel, C. Shore, G. Feldman and S. Lathrop (2005) 'Toward an Anthropology of Public Policy' In: *Annals of the American Academy of Political and Social Science* 600, 30–51

M. Wesołek (2012) Komentarz In: *Gazeta Wyborcza. Dodatek Poznański*, no. 222. 7646, 22–23.09.2012, 4

M. Wesołek (2013) 'Lech zapłaci miastu mniej. Na stadionie za osiemset milionów Poznań nie zarobi' In: *Gazeta Wyborcza. Dodatek Poznański* 14.05.2013, 1

M. Wesołek and M. Wybieralski (2012) 'Stadion tylko dla Lecha' In: *Gazeta Wyborcza. Dodatek Poznański*, no. 222. 7646, 22–23.09.2012, 1

D. Whitson and J. Horne (2006) 'Underestimated Costs and Overestimated Benefits? Comparing the Outcomes of Sports Mega-Events in Canada and Japan' In: J. Horne and W. Manzenreiter (eds.) *The Sociological Review. Special Issue: Sociological Review Monograph Series: Sports Mega-Events: Social Scientific Analyses of a Global Phenomenon* 54, Supplement s2, 71–89

D. Whitson and D. Macintosh (1993) 'Becoming a World-Class City: Hallmark Events and Sport Franchises in the Growth Strategies of Western Canadian Cities' In: *Sociology of Sport Journal* 10, 221–40

Wieloletnia prognoza finansowa miasta (2016) Materiały Urzędu Miasta Poznania

J. Wilczak (2012) 'Pustadiony' In: *Polityka*, nr 20. 2858, 16–22.05.2012, 64–5

J. Wilkin (2013) 'Dlaczego ekonomia straciła duszę?' In: *Gazeta Wyborcza. Magazyn Świąteczny*, no. 297. 8026, 21–22.12.2013, 28–9

R. Williams (1973) *The Country and the City*. London: Hogarth

R. Williams (1977) *Marxism and Literature*. Oxford: Blackwell

R. Williams (1983) *Culture and Society 1780–1950*. New York: Columbia University Press

M. Wojtczuk (2012) 'Milionowe straty Stadionu Narodowego' In: *Gazeta Wyborcza*, no. 298. 7723, 21.12.2012, 6

E. R. Wolf (1982) *Europe and the People Without History*. Berkeley: University of California Press

W. Woźniak (2013) 'Sport Mega-Events and the Need for Critical Sociological Research: The Case of Euro 2012' In: *Sociological Review (Przegląd Socjologiczny)*, no. 3/2013, 31–50

M. Wybieralski (2011) 'Grobelizm, czyli tak się rządzi w Poznaniu' In: *Gazeta Wyborcza. Dodatek Poznański* 1.07.2011, http://poznan.gazeta.pl/poznan/1,36037,7047791,Grobelizm__czyli_tak_sie_rzadzi_w_Poznaniu.html, date accessed 28.01.2017

J. Żakowski (2014) 'Słowo wstępne. Wszyscy będziemy prekariuszami' In: G. Standing (ed.) *Prekariat. Nowa niebezpieczna klasa*. Warszawa: Wydawnictwo Naukowe PWN SA, 9–20 [Polish translation of G. Standing (2011), *The Precariat: The New Dangerous Class*. Bloomsbury Publishing Plc.]

J. Ziółkowski (1967) (ed.) *Poznań. Społeczno-przestrzenne skutki industrializacji*. Warszawa: Państwowe Wydawnictwo Naukowe

F. Znaniecki (1931) 'Group Crisis Produced by Voluntary Undertakings' In K. Young (ed.) *Social Attitudes*. New York: Henry Holt, 265–90, http://www.brocku.ca/MeadProject/Young/1931/11_Znaniecki.html, date accessed 28.01.2017

F. Znaniecki and J. Ziółkowski (1984) *Czym jest dla Ciebie miasto Poznań? Dwa konkursy: 1928/1964*. Warszawa, Poznań: Państwowe Wydawnictwo Naukowe

S. Zukin (1991) *Landscapes of Power: From Detroit to Disney World*. Berkeley: University of California Press

P. Zych (2013) 'Futbolowy plan Marshalla nie wypalił. Rok po Euro' In: *Przegląd Sportowy* 17.VI, no 139 (16 612), 6–7

P. Żytnicki (2012) 'Piłkarski klub nie reguluje swoich rachunków, więc... POSiR płaci za Lecha' In: *Gazeta Wyborcza. Dodatek poznański* 8–9.12.2012, 1

Index

© The Author(s) 2017
M.Z. Kowalska, *Urban Politics of a Sporting Mega Event*,
Football Research in an Enlarged Europe,
DOI 10.1007/978-3-319-52105-3

Printed by Printforce, the Netherlands